Quiet Moments for Busy Moms

❀

Linda McNatt Page and Rebecca Gentry Mulvaney

VINE
BOOKS

SERVANT PUBLICATIONS
ANN ARBOR, MICHIGAN

Vine Books is an imprint of Servant Publications especially designed to serve evangelical Christians.

All Scripture quotations, except as otherwise noted, are taken from the HOLY BIBLE, NEW INTERNATIONAL VERSION®. © 1973, 1978, 1984 by International Bible Society. Used by permission of Zondervan Publishing House. All rights reserved.

The stories in this book are true and have been freely shared with the authors and used by permission of the individuals involved. In a few cases, pseudonyms have been used to protect privacy.

Published by Servant Publications
P.O. Box 8617
Ann Arbor, Michigan 48107

Cover design: Paz Design Group, Salem, Oregon
Cover photograph: © Michael Melford, Inc. / Image Bank

00 01 02 03 10 9 8 7 6 5 4 3 2 1

Printed in the United States of America
ISBN 1-56955-196-0

LIBRARY OF CONGRESS CATALOGING-IN-PUBLICATION DATA

Page, Linda McNatt, 1953-
     Quiet moments for busy moms : Linda McNatt Page and Rebecca Gentry
     Mulvaney.
        p.   cm.
     ISBN 1-56955-196-0 (alk. paper)
     1. Mothers—Religious life.   I. Mulvaney, Rebecca Gentry.   II. Title.

BV4529.P34 2000
242'.6431—dc21   00-036341

To Martha, Beverly, Aurelia, Jessie, Minnie, Bethany,
Benjamin, Jeffrey, and Michael.

This book is dedicated to the mothers who have
mothered us and the children we have mothered.
From them we have learned immeasurably about
the joys and failures, the ministry and struggles,
the love, heart, and soul of motherhood.

The Story of Two Busy Moms

Two women sit in a booth in the local Burger King. Extra-large drinks sit before them, dripping cold condensation. Laughter occasionally bounces between them, rippling its way to the ceiling. For the most part, however, the conversation seems serious, as though the words passing between them create a lifeline. Heads nod in silent agreement. Eyes lock tentatively, and then glances drop to the tabletop. The facial expressions of these women show comfort, acceptance, and above all hope. This might appear to be a rendezvous of old friends, but this isn't old. It is new. It is a beginning.

The demographics of the two find them to be an unlikely pair. Bekah is tall, blond, and thin. Linda is short, strawberry-brunette, and not thin. Bekah has lived all over the United States, moving wherever her husband's corporate position has taken them. Linda is a hometown girl married to a hometown boy who owns his own small business. At the time of this meeting, Bekah's children are in high school. Linda's are in elementary and middle school. Bekah finished college but never went to work. Linda started her first job one week after completing her degree and has worked ever since. Bekah's days are filled with volunteer work, while Linda teaches special education at the neighborhood elementary school. Bekah is an extrovert, a real people-person. In contrast, being with people takes a lot of energy for Linda. Bekah has friends all over the country. Linda seems to know everyone in town. It's a "you say po-tay-to and I say po-tah-to" kind of thing.

This beginning at Burger King marked the end of a season of

loneliness for both of them. These two hours of talking and enough Diet Coke to float the Titanic became the prologue to a friendship that for Bekah and Linda would be unique.

In spite of their exterior differences they are soul mates in heart issues. They share a common interest in running, something Linda had left on the delivery table since her second son's birth. They share a common lifelong love for music, applying their love to leading others in worship: Bekah on keys and reading the music, Linda on strings and "playing by ear"—the one with the voice and real talent.

Bekah and Linda have undertaken a number of projects during their friendship, the most telling of which was the writing of Linda's first book. With the publishing contract signed and deadline set, Bekah haltingly offered to edit and critique Linda's writing. "If you think our friendship can handle it," she said.

"We can handle it," Linda replied. "Besides, I really need you." And the writing of a book became another tie between the two.

As Bekah began her speaking career, Linda became her sounding board, letting her thoughts come alive as they took long therapeutic walks—a wide-open, verbal, editing process.

After the first book's success, publishers approached Linda and Bekah about co-authoring a second book, this one for mothers. This time the critique went both ways, and the friendship only flourished through days and hours of wordsmithing on the porch swing over iced tea and laughter.

Readers will become familiar with these two busy women's lives through this book. They will likely recognize two different voices. When curious about whose heart is being shared, the reader can check the initials on each entry. Finally, readers will doubtless notice this book is uniquely flavored by a divinely connected friendship between the authors.

Matters Too Great

Congratulations, Mrs. Mulvaney. You're pregnant."

A river swelled behind my eyes and flowed down my face. These weren't tears of joy—not yet anyway. Neither were they tears of dread. These were tears of awe. I couldn't quite wrap my mind around the idea of the creation of life within me.

From that moment on, my life wasn't my own. I couldn't direct the healthy growth of life within my belly, nor dictate its effect on my swelling form. These were matters too great for me to control.

Once the baby was born, I had plenty of other concerns. What if she gets sick? What if her development isn't normal? What if she doesn't awaken? I wasn't a worrier, as mothers go, but my mother-heart couldn't help wondering what dangers lurked ahead for our little one. I could protect her from many but not all of life's perils. Such matters were too great for a mother's protective efforts.

Every morning, as I launched my kids off to another school day, I told them I loved them and watched as they trudged with loaded backpacks toward the bus stop. I wondered if they would return to me later that afternoon. I could worry about an out-of-control vehicle hitting them on their way to the bus stop, or a school bus accident, or violence at school. Instead I released my children to God's care. Their days were filled with matters too great for my sphere of influence.

Carefully I guided my children. I taught them about their vulnerabilities, so they wouldn't risk their own safety unnecessarily. But I couldn't save them from all harm.

They rode home from school with friends; I couldn't prevent

them from being in an accident. They went out on dates; I couldn't control teenage hormones. They went to arenas for concerts and games; I couldn't dictate what others in the crowd might do. Matters were definitely out of my hands.

Waving good-bye to my children as they drove to faraway college towns was a helpless feeling. Far from my reach, my children struggled with temptation, sickness, fatigue, finances, unreasonable teachers, challenging relationships, and consequences of unwise choices. My heart wanted to rush to their rescue, but I did the only thing I could when matters were too great. I prayed.

Now my children are embarking on their adult journeys. From the beginning I've known little control, but I've been far from powerless. I've known the power of being well-acquainted with the Ruler of the universe. He commands the angels who guard my children, and he rules over every event in their lives. No, I don't worry—though it could come quite naturally for my mother-heart. Instead I remind myself of the One who is in control, the One who loves my children even more than I do, the One who knows what is best. *These* are matters too great for me!

> I do not concern myself with great matters or things too wonderful for me. But I have stilled and quieted my soul; like a weaned child with its mother, like a weaned child is my soul within me. O [mothers], put your hope in the Lord both now and forevermore.
>
> PSALM 131:1b-3

RGM

Just Wait

I guess I heard the words of impending doom and misery most often when my boys were little. I wondered at the time why on earth I'd decided to have children if every milestone meant my life would be harder. You've heard their voices too. They're the naysayers, the doom-and-gloomers. I call them the just-waiters.

For many of us, our first just-waiter was our mothers using what we now know to be a less-than-desirable parenting technique: "Just wait till your father gets home." Oh, how miserable life would be when the man of the house arrived to inflict pain and punishment. Poor Dad. He unknowingly was given the task of proving just how horrible life could be on the other side of "just wait." His unsuspecting children, on the other hand, were being set up for a lifetime of encounters with "just-waiters."

When I was growing up, a few "just-waiters" were always in the grades ahead of me. Just wait till you have to do long division! Just wait till next year when you have homework every night! Just wait till you have Mr. Crankypants for Chemistry I!

But the greatest flood of just-waiters enters our lives when we embark upon this journey called motherhood. They start almost immediately. Just wait till you take that baby home and have to get up with him a hundred times a night. Just wait till she's teething! Just wait till he's crawling. Just wait till she's walking. Just wait till you have two in diapers. Just wait till potty training. Just wait till they're teenagers! Just wait till they start driving. Just wait till you have to find a college. A-a-a-a-k! Where can I find a tomorrow worth waiting for?

I want to enjoy my present, not just endure it. The present is to be my teacher and my pleasure, not an hourglass to be watched with dread of doom. Somehow at our house, we've survived those formidable stages foretold by the just-waiters. We've potty trained and bottle broken. We've taken away the pacifier and the training wheels. We've learned to crawl, walk, and drive. We stand on the threshold of more just-wait times. Just wait till he graduates! Just wait till you have to drive away from his college campus for the first time.

Just wait? I believe I will just wait. I believe I'll wait all day long today. I'll revel in the joys of this phase of my relationship with my children. I believe I'll just wait and see what tomorrow brings.

I wait for the Lord, my soul waits, and in His word, I put my hope.
PSALM 130:5

LMP

Bekah's Excellent Adventure

Safaris. Mountain climbs. Going into the wilds where few have gone before. These are the mental images summoned by the word *adventure*. But an adventure is, in fact, going anywhere someone hasn't gone before—or doing anything someone hasn't done before. New territory! As a grown woman, I'm afraid I've grown less adventuresome. I've become comfortable with the known territory and experiences that yield expected outcomes. I've settled for "safe," avoiding the "wildness" of new ventures. Several summers ago, however, I began an adventure that hasn't ended yet.

As I searched for spiritual nourishment for those "lazy, hazy days of summer," I found an interesting workbook called a "fifty-day spiritual adventure."* Hmmm, I thought; I haven't been on an adventure for a long time.

Among other aspects of the study I was instructed to look for daily "God-sightings." That sounded more like something to do with storm-chasing or UFOs. Rather than looking for funnel clouds and lights in the night sky, I was to keep an eagle-eye out for "sightings" of God's activity in my day-to-day life. Of course, I already believed God was active in this world and in my life, but I didn't realize how little I recognized his presence.

I began noticing obvious answers to prayer and unexpected evidences of his care. I perceived unusual linkages between events and their timing. I began to discern his help and assistance when I was doing those things which would be considered "ministry" or "God's work." Every day for fifty days I was to write down at least one God-sighting. At first, it was difficult. But, after a bit of practice, I "saw" him everywhere. I saw his hand in the friendships he provided. I felt his presence as he helped me understand my child's struggle or gave me words to help my husband who was overwhelmed with his job. I recognized the way he used me to encourage others and the way he, through others, encouraged me!

I noticed how God was helping my son overcome timidity and growing my little girl into a reflective young woman. When my daughter said she examined her motives as she dressed for a date, I knew God was shaping her spirit. When my son showed compassion for the kid who finished last in the cross-country meet, I thanked God for the work he'd done in his heart.

As I daily journaled the goodness I saw and experienced, I found I'd embarked on a journey toward personal richness. You see, "the God hunt" became for me a new way of thinking—an adventurous way of living. That summer, the God-hunt unleashed the adventurer in me, yielding a thankful heart and a hopeful spirit. Who knows? Perhaps—just over the next mountain of laundry, beyond the next valley of the mundane—a God-sighting awaits!

I will meditate on all your works and consider all your mighty deeds.

PSALM 77:12

RGM

---

* *Daring to Dream Again: Breaking Through Barriers That Hold Us Back* (Wheaton, Ill.: Chapel of the Air Ministries, 1993).

Morning Stars

Morning is my favorite time of day. I really should take advantage more often of all that is offered by the dawn of a new day. One fall morning I took it all in. Dawn was a thin pink line across the eastern sky as I stepped outside. My fingers laced around my coffee cup. Steam warmed my face. An autumn breeze gave my cheek a good morning kiss, hinting that something magnificent was about to happen.

I've often wondered what it must have sounded like when the morning stars sang together. Job tells us they sang as our divine builder was laying the cornerstone of the earth. With his majestic trowel in hand, God began his creation to the accompaniment of angelic singing. Were there words to this chorus? Surely God's wondrous creative power was too incomprehensible for words. Surely awestruck angels could only pierce the silence of heaven with unspoken harmony.

I stood statue-still that autumn morning, letting earth's gentle breath bathe me. Creation slowly opened its eyes from the squint of predawn. That's when I heard it. Music. Undefined instrumentation, no lyrics. Voices? Instruments? What was it? Was it the breeze in the pine trees? A distant wind chime? The mystery of harmonious discord surrounded me. I couldn't locate it. I could only experience its soothing presence, listen to its whistling whisper. Maybe, just maybe, the morning stars were singing heaven's fanfare to the day. Maybe, just this once, I was intruding upon a heavenly morning ritual. Maybe the Bright and Morning Star himself was greeting me and holding me in his embrace. With head thrown back, I filled my lungs with freshness, my ears with symphony, and my spirit with

Presence. The sun made her connection with the earth, flooding me with warmth and promise. Birds added descant to the music of heaven, and I was lifted up.

I didn't want to relinquish my heavenly connection that morning, but earthbound matters called me back to my life. That day somehow was a little brighter than most, my mind a little fresher, my heart a little lighter. My day had been blessed by a Morning Star beginning.

The morning stars sang together.

JOB 38:7

LMP

Handprints

Scurrying through the house, I made last-minute preparations for the evening's dinner party. Our "community" group from church was coming over, and everyone would bring a dish to share, so it shouldn't be much trouble. I silently went through my checklist. Vacuum. Clean bathrooms. Set tables. Make coffee. Everything was looking good—except for the smudges on the hallway wall. Why do kids have to touch every wall they pass, as if to verify it's real and not an optical illusion?

My life is too full, I told myself. When would I ever have time to paint the hall? Next year? I doubted it. And what about the piles of unread magazines, missions newsletters, school publications, and articles of interest waiting to be filed? They seemed at home nested on their corner of my kitchen desk. All of it is worthwhile. All of it deserves to be read. When would I ever get through it? Probably not in this decade!

The perfectionist in me was frustrated and overwhelmed. In God's perfect timing I "happened" to be working through a Bible study on the stresses of life when I came to the chapter on time pressures. After studying how Jesus invested his time, I identified his lifelong priorities. What would it look like if his priorities actually became my priorities?

My next task was to keep an hourly journal of how I spent my time for one week. It was easy to see where my time went. Carpooling. Studying for and leading a Bible study. Taking my kids to practices, games, and lessons. Getting together with friends. Visiting with neighbors and other parents. Housecleaning (kept to a minimum). Helping with homework. Hosting my community group.

tudy workbook then challenged me to see how
aligned with Jesus' (and my) priorities. Was I
my whole being (Mt 22:37)? Was I loving oth-
(Mt 22:39)? Was I "shining my light" into the world (Mt
5:16)? Was I making disciples (Mt 28:19-20)? Was I striving to
be holy (1 Tm 4:7-8)? Was I providing for those entrusted to
my care (1 Tm 5:8)? Was I doing excellent work for the Lord
(Col 3:23)?

Imagine my surprise to see no mention of smudged hallways
or piles on kitchen counters. It was affirming that I was indeed
making choices aligned with the priorities I professed to live by.
Suddenly I realized the handprints on the walls were a testi-
mony to what was really important in my life—God and people.
Ever since that time, whenever I'm tempted to let worldly
imperfections steal my joy, I simply remember those little dirty
handprints. Handprints that spoke of my lifelong priorities.

"Love the Lord your God with all your heart and with all your soul
and with all your mind and with all your strength." The second is
this: "Love your neighbor as yourself." There is no commandment
greater than these.

MARK 12:30-31

RGM

The Stones Cry Out!

Jerusalem was teeming with people preparing to celebrate the Passover. As many as a million celebrants would crowd into the Holy City each year to observe the most sacred of all Jewish holidays. People walked shoulder-to-shoulder on the narrow streets. Households spilled over with guests. Campfires dotted the hills, courtyards, and alleys.

Year after year Roman soldiers managed the dense crowds, but this year held an additional problem. This man, Jesus, would be coming to town with his motley brood of disciples. Outrageous rumors about him were flying around the city. They said that by his touch, lepers were healed; by his words, the lame walked and the blind could see. But now the city was buzzing with the news that this Jesus had raised Lazarus from the dead. Lazarus had been dead four days, his body wrapped and laid in a tomb. At Jesus' command, Lazarus stood and walked out of the tomb, alive. Everyone in town wanted to catch a glimpse of the man whose words had power over life and death.

Jesus entered Jerusalem riding on a donkey, a symbol of peace, but his presence created chaos. People were shouting, waving palm branches, and running in circles around him. Was this the One who would come and set them free? Was he their hope, their deliverer? Annoyed religious leaders stood back watching with crossed arms and raised eyebrows. This joyful abandonment was more than they could take.

"Teacher," they said to him, "rebuke your disciples!"

"I tell you," he replied, "if they keep silent, the stones will cry out!"

There is a Truth whose mouth will not be shut. The enemies of Jesus tried on that triumphal day to silence the effect of his presence, but it would not be quieted. Within a few days the people's voices would betray him, but stones would cry out. The shouting began with a single gigantic stone rolled away from a tomb, pulsing the message, "He is not here. He is risen!" Later, stones that pounded the life from martyrs lay in bloodied stillness and shouted, "He is worth dying for!" The temple's fallen stones lay just as he said—not one upon another. "He knew!" was their message.

Not so long ago, hot coffee and warm conversation filled the kitchen as I visited with an old friend from college. We laughed as we revisited the antics of our misspent youth. As she showed me around her new home, I noticed, on the hutch in her dining room, a rock about the size of the palm of my hand. "What's this?" I asked, picking it up and stroking its smoothness.

Her face became serious. "That's my heart of stone," she said. "Christ replaced it with a heart of flesh, but I keep this one to remind me."

There is a Truth whose mouth will not be shut. The stones are crying out!

"I tell you," he replied, "if they keep quiet, the stones will cry out."

LUKE 19:40

LMP

Heaven on My Block

D on't throw sand, Jenny!"

"We don't allow spitting, Mark!"

"No pushing people off the swings, Billy!"

It seemed I was constantly correcting the neighborhood children who came to play in our backyard. I didn't mind our backyard being the neighborhood playground, but somehow these kids would have to play by our rules.

"Johnny, that word isn't allowed in our yard!"

"We don't call each other bad names, Tamara!"

I quickly realized I had too many rules. How could I expect three-, four-, and five-year-olds to remember my list of statutes? As I pondered over simplifying my backyard government for these children, I thought of one simple rule.

"We have only one rule in our yard," I announced one day. "To be loving and kind." The children looked blankly at me. Perhaps I should see if these little ones understood.

"Is it loving and kind to throw sand?"

"Noooo!" they said in unison.

"Is it loving and kind to spit at each other?"

"Noooo!" they crooned.

"Is it loving and kind to push people off the swings?"

"Noooo!"

These little folk who had never attended Sunday school *did* know about love and kindness. I had struck a chord—an understandable one.

"If you don't obey this one rule," I continued, "you'll have to leave this yard for the day. That's our rule. Tell it to any other children who come to play in our yard."

The kids seemed refreshed that this yard had only one rule, and over the summer I could hear them reminding each other of "the rule." One day, through my open kitchen window, I overheard my own four-year-old initiating a newcomer to the yard with a sandbox lecture.

"Is it loving and kind to call names?"

"No."

"Is it loving and kind to say bad words?"

"No."

As the summer progressed, more and more neighborhood kids chose to play daily in our backyard. It had something others didn't. Children found they were treated with respect. They didn't have conflicts. They didn't have to fight for a turn on the swings or the slide. They didn't have to defend themselves.

Whenever the rule was broken—and, yes, of course, it sometimes was—I would calmly escort the misbehaving child out through the fence-gate. I would sympathize that they had to leave our yard, but I encouraged them to come back the next day if they would behave in a loving and kind way. Usually the child would cry, because leaving this yard meant going back out into the real world. The real world where people yell mean things at you, do mean things, and generally don't act loving and kind.

Without realizing it, I had provided a safe haven for these children. Perhaps it was their first glimpse of heaven. I hope they'll remember what a difference love makes.

Be kind and compassionate to one another.

EPHESIANS 4:32

RGM

20

God-Sighting at Pringles Park

Bekah has written about the summer of the "God hunt." She told of how she spent that summer reporting "God sightings," learning to look for God in all the right places. I, too, was a member of that summer safari. I was also amazed and astounded by God's daily, hourly, moment-by-moment interruption of my insistence upon running my own life.

Such was the case one summer night at Pringles Park, home field for my hometown's minor league baseball team. I made the difficult choice to miss one of Michael's games to go to my first Diamond Jaxx game with the Mulvaneys and Bekah's parents. Entertainment, good company, good seats. What a deal! I knew I was going for a relaxing evening. What I didn't know was that I was going on another safari.

As the mother of a pitcher and a catcher, I know that the best seats in the house are those behind home plate, and our tickets led us exactly there. Diet Pepsi in hand, best seats in the house, surrounded by friends, ball game before me, I was happy. Not for long. The Mulvaneys soon spotted friends on the third-base line.

"Come on down here. There are plenty of seats!" their friends pleaded. But they didn't understand. I was behind home plate. I had my Diet Pepsi. I was happy. I was comfortable ... I was compliant ... I was moving.

Just as I settled into my new location and decided all would be well, someone tapped me on the shoulder.

"Hey, Mrs. Page."

I looked up to see a six-foot, tow-headed young man I hadn't seen since he left my classroom as a fifth-grader. He was grinning from ear to ear. In shock I called out his name and felt a smile spread across my face. For the next six innings he filled me in on the last ten years of his life.

The last I'd heard of him, he was in trouble in high school and had left town to go and live with his dad. He told me of his struggles in and out of school. He told me of an accidental shooting that nearly took his life. He told me he'd discovered God was taking care of him all along. This once-troubled young man had just come back from a Promise Keepers weekend.

The Jaxx won the game that night, and God scored a direct hit in my heart. Sometimes the Holy Spirit whispers to me: "Linda, it's OK. Go to the Jaxx game tonight." This time he dragged me from behind home plate, away from my comfort zone, on safari to Section H. Sometimes he just insists on being God, whether I like it or not. Sometimes he just shows up whether I'm looking or not. A God-sighting was waiting for me on the third-base line at the Diamond Jaxx game. God had, for me, the best seat in the house.

> Great are the works of the Lord; they are pondered by all who delight in them.
>
> PSALM 111:2

LMP

My Mind's Ear

When I was little, my grandmother gave me a conch shell—you know, those shells most people instinctively hold up to their ears. Having grown up in Missouri, I hadn't seen many shells, and I marveled at this one's size and bumpy texture. As I explored its various points with my little-girl hand, my grandmother smiled as if she had a special secret to tell me.

"Hold it next to your ear. You'll hear the ocean," she whispered as if she and I were the only ones privileged to share this mystery of nature. I looked at her in disbelief. Both my mother and grandmother were grand teasers, and I was usually gullible enough to believe their incredible stories. But this time I was wary. I would look pretty silly putting this big shell up to my ear—especially expecting to hear the sound of waves captured within.

"Really!" my grandmother prodded. "Put it up to your ear." She seemed genuine enough. So I raised the shell to my ear, and I heard the roar of the sea for the very first time. So *this* is what the ocean sounds like! (And I was none the wiser until I heard the rhythmic, crashing surf for myself on my honeymoon.) My treasured shell remained on my dresser for many years—the ocean's music at my fingertips.

The woman who taught me to listen to shells can no longer hear the ocean's roar. She can no longer hear the harmony of a symphony or the music of conversation. But, in her world of silence, sounds live on in memory. Just as my conch had captured the sound of the surf, her mind has captured the sounds of her lifetime. Her children's giggles. The screen door slamming. Her husband calling her name from the garden. The intertwining of her voice with his as they ended each day with the Lord's Prayer. I know she hears such sounds—no hearing aids necessary.

I sometimes wonder what sounds will still be heard in my mind's ear, if someday the sound waves of my world go unperceived. I think I shall enjoy sounds of a lifetime kept alive in my head.

Nighttime cricket symphonies. The squeak of the porch swing. The whisper of the wind in the pine trees. The innocent contented sound of my little girl, humming as she serves invisible tea to her dollies. Happy voices of children as they play in the sandbox outside my kitchen window. Such is the music of my life, music finer and dearer to me than any composed by Bach or Handel, music captured in my mind and heart that will accompany me a lifetime.

But Mary treasured up all these things and pondered them in her heart.

LUKE 2:19

RGM

Lost Viking

The note read, "Mom, gone to be a lost Viking behind the house where the big dog lives." I stared at the note in amazement. Somewhere on the short bike ride from our house to the "house where the big dog lives," my eleven-year-old son would transform in soul, mind, and purpose into a "lost Viking." He would see what a lost Viking sees, hear what a lost Viking hears, and think only as a lost Viking.

I'm excited first that there remains in my son a remnant of creativity inextinguishable by the lure of technology. Today he has chosen "make believe" over TV or the beeps and boops of electronic games. He will, by his choice, unlock his imagination. He doesn't even know that, in so doing, he is helping his soul to be more teachable, his spirit more pliable. If he can unlock his imagination for play, then it can also be opened for learning. His day, even as a youngster, will be filled with soft, teachable moments.

Jesus taught in parables, unlocking imaginations and pouring truth into teachable moments. When I read the parable of the prodigal son, I become him. I smell the pigpen, I feel the dust on my feet, and I long for the house of my Father. When I read of the workers in the vineyard, I think of exhausting long days in the hot summer sun. I can wrap my heart around the gratitude of the workers who worked only an hour and the frustration of those who labored all day. When I hear the parable of the good Samaritan, I want so much to be him, but I see so much of myself in those who walked away.

Lecture and logic cannot take me to a pigpen, a vineyard, or a lonely roadway. Logic may teach me facts, even truth, but it doesn't make my spirit soft. So it is with our children. Open imaginations give way to pliable, teachable souls. So there will be a twinkle in my eye when my lost Viking returns. He will have much to tell me. And in that teachable moment with me, he will have much to learn.

Then he told them many things in parables.

MATTHEW 13:3

LMP

One Choice at a Time

The alarm goes off. I face the first choice of my day—to hit the snooze button or abandon the warm lair of my bed. It's only the first of hundreds of choices my day holds. I choose to snooze—due to last night's choice to stay up too late.

Bagel or muffin?

Butter or cream cheese?

Eat in the car or skip it altogether?

Groggily I'm bombarded by a steady onslaught of choices now. They show no mercy for my fragile early-morning condition. I'm beginning to pay for my first choice of the day. Now I haven't the time or patience to choose between the clothes in my closet. I hate running late.

Moments later, I choose sarcasm over graciousness when my daughter can't find her volleyball uniform. I choose to rant and rave in traffic, rather than decelerate. I'm off to a perilous start to my day, with its own set of unique and unpredictable choices.

At midmorning, I must decide whether to invite a troubled young woman from my Bible study to have lunch with me or skip lunch to run some errands I didn't have time for earlier this morning. Since I skipped breakfast, I'd better not skip lunch. I wonder how long I'll pay for those few minutes under the "snooze button."

I congratulate myself after lunch for making a good choice. My friend needed the encouragement; I needed the nourishment. I should have passed on the fries.

Like a locomotive going down a mountain without brakes, the choices pick up steam as the day progresses, challenging me every few seconds.

Paper or plastic? Cash or charge?

More choices assault me with requests from my offspring, the discovery of homework not done, and a note from a teacher sending a red flag. Even more important than what I *do* is how I *respond*. Like an invasion of an army, the bombardment of choices sends me hiding like a frightened child behind my closed bedroom door.

Momentarily escaping insistent demands of more choices, I sit on the floor beside my bed. I remind myself that, with all of their mind-muddling confusion, choices are a gift. Amazingly, God trusts *me* with choices—choices weighted with the power to demean or esteem or even destroy.

Suddenly, the redemptive quality built into the nature of choice-making becomes clear. Each choice stands alone. Sure, I make bad choices—like choosing french fries instead of steamed broccoli. Sure, there are consequences. But, in less than sixty seconds, another choice will loom before me, and I'll have the opportunity to make a wise choice, regardless of how badly I blew the last one. Does a wise choice cancel out the consequences of the bad choice? No. But neither does a bad choice sentence me to a life of unwise choices. I forgive myself. I live life one choice at a time. I open the bedroom door, ready to re-enter my world of choice-living, determined to make the next one wise.

Be very careful, then, how you live—not as unwise but as wise, making the most of every opportunity, because the days are evil.

EPHESIANS 5:15-16

RGM

The Rhythm of Life

❀

Rhythm has been a part of creation since the beginning: "And there was evening, and there was morning—the first day." Sunrise, sunset—rhythm. The tide flows in, retreats, flows in, retreats—rhythm. We expect the world to have a rhythm. We need our lives to flow with a rhythm. Though predictable, rhythm isn't mundane. It is the wondrous ebb and flow of life. It's something you can count on, plan on, know. The rhythm is in the knowing.

So it is with relationships. The rhythm is in the knowing. Last week an elderly couple was seated across from me in a doctor's waiting room. The rhythm of their relationship so intrigued me that I couldn't help but watch them. They sat almost snuggled together exchanging toothless smiles. He patted her knee. She rubbed his arm. They said little, but I saw her lips form the words, "I love you." When their name was called, he stood and, taking her purse in one hand and her elbow in the other, gently lifted her to her feet. They shuffled as one toward the waiting nurse. No words, just rhythm. The rhythm is in the knowing.

My friendship with Bekah provides rhythm in my life. Even when we go for a walk, the rhythm of our friendship is evident. It's in the knowing. I get tired, and without a word she slows her pace. We do a turn; as she swings wide, I stay inside. We get home. I collapse; she pours iced tea. I sit on the blue couch; she sits on the floor. The rhythm is in the knowing.

Sometimes we have to deal with the loss of rhythm. I remember the afternoon Bekah and I were sitting on my front porch drinking iced tea. I sensed a tension, a sadness in her, but said nothing. Finally as she was preparing to leave, she told me her husband had accepted a job transfer. She would be moving in a few months. With the adjustments and changes her leaving means, I know there will be no disruption of the heart, no loss of connection. We will e-mail, snail-mail, fly, and phone. I will miss her "change into your walkin' clothes and get over here" phone calls. I will miss our stress-relief trips for a giant diet soda, our walks, our talks, our time together. I will miss the rhythm. But we will have a new one. "See you in two weeks." "Meet you in Arkansas." "Let's fly to Seattle!" We'll always have a rhythm, for the rhythm is in the knowing.

You know when I sit and when I rise; you perceive my thoughts from afar. You discern my going out and my lying down; you are familiar with all my ways.

PSALM 139:2-3

LMP

"I Kin Ye"

Little Tree knew when he heard Granpa say to Granma, "I kin ye, Bonnie Bee," he meant, "I love you," for the feeling was in the words. To his Cherokee grandparents, love and understanding were synonymous. They believed it was impossible to love someone (even God) without first understanding him. Granpa explained that originally "kinfolks" meant any folks you understood—or "loved folks." Only later did it come to mean simply blood relatives. *The Education of Little Tree,** Forrest Carter's tale of his Appalachian childhood, is in itself an education in love and understanding.

As a mom, I find that Little Tree was right. Love at its best is interwoven with understanding. As I seek to understand the "kinfolk" living under my roof, I often find myself helping them understand themselves.

Benji was four and a serious Matchbox car driver. He hated to be interrupted from his intense road-building in the dirt for Mom's errands and especially for Mom's daily outing to practice the pipe organ at church. The whining began as soon as I gave the five-minute warning of the estimated departure time.

In the annoying pitch that only a four-year-old can produce, Benji protested in elongated siren-sounding protests. "Do I have to go? Why do I have to go? I don't wanna go!" After packing up forty of his favorite Matchbox cars, the chorus would continue all the way to the church.

I could expect this scenario every time I practiced the organ. Normally I tried to explain (in preschooler terms) why this excursion was necessary. But one afternoon I tried a new approach to Benji's tantrum.

"You're crying because you're upset with Mom for making you go to the church with her, aren't you, Benji?"

"Uh-huh," he offered through his angry sobs.

"You wish you could stay at home and play with your toys."

"Uh-huh," his blubbering seemed to be less furious.

"It makes you mad that Mom drags you away from your toys for her to go practice the organ."

The whimpering dissipated. The angry little tyrant in the backseat was transformed into a contented little man. Understanding himself and being understood diffused his anger and brought contentment. Though my four-year-old son was unable to wrap words around his undeniable emotion, I could do that for him. He needed me for that. He needed to know I understood—that I "kinned" him.

Since that day I've had a clearer picture of my role as one who understands and guides my children to understand themselves. When you think about it, love and understanding are all we really want. It's a gift I can give—to my children, my husband, my friends. I can because I "kin" them.

The purposes of a man's heart are deep waters, but a [woman] of understanding draws them out.

PROVERBS 20:5

RGM

*Forrest Carter, *The Education of Little Tree* (Albuquerque, N.M.: University of New Mexico Press, 1976), 38.

Fruit-Faced

Tennessee summers can be stifling. As I was growing up in the fifties and sixties, finding relief from summer's thick, muggy enclosure wasn't always easy. Our once-a-year pilgrimage to a pick-your-own peach orchard was just the ticket for an afternoon of breezy coolness. Walking in the shade of fruit-laden branches brought welcome refreshment. But it wasn't nearly as welcome as filling my mouth with the juicy sweetness of a fresh, soft peach. I remember watching my grandmother select from our basket a fuzzy delicacy and turn to offer me what I knew would be the pick-of-the-peck. At least one peach would never make it out of the orchard. Holding it between thumb and finger, I bent over at the waist and began my fruit-feast with passion. Ah, yes, wet-faced, elbow-dripping delight.

I think of those delightful peaches as I read what the Bible says about fruit. Jesus tells us God is glorified when his followers bear much fruit. Fruit-bearing shows we are Jesus' disciples. Our lives are to be like fruit-heavy branches, bowing and dipping in the summer breeze. The sweet core of the fruit of the Spirit is love, love that drips juicy with joy, peace, patience, kindness, goodness, faithfulness, gentleness, and self-control. Life in the Spirit—bearing sweet, delicious fruit—means loving fully and well. Jesus said, "I chose you and appointed you to bear fruit—fruit that will last." Love-fruit never fails.

Sometimes I try to imagine God strolling through his orchard, refreshed by its coolness and glorying in its beauty. Every soul belonging to Christ is a branch in this orchard. Its vastness meets the horizon, and yet God knows the story of every life represented. He knows when each branch sprang from the tree and how each fruit came to be. When he comes to your branch, may he find you weighted down with plump, tender fruit. Perhaps he'll ponder the right choice for his enjoyment. His glory lights every shadow of the orchard as he walks away in wet-faced, elbow-dripping delight.

But the fruit of the Spirit is love, joy, peace, patience, kindness, goodness, faithfulness, gentleness, and self-control.

GALATIANS 5:22-23

LMP

Pray Naked

❀

I hadn't slept in a college dorm for a very long time. I'd forgotten about the nocturnal cacophony of excited voices in the hall, stereo music, slamming doors, and occasional tearful sobbing over a broken heart. My first night in the top bunk of my daughter Bethany's "loft" was practically sleepless. I heard the comings and goings of female night creatures until the morning light winked through the window.

As the sun rose higher, the dorm seemed to be going to sleep. But my internal clock (obviously in a different time zone from these nineteen-year-olds) told me it was time to get up. I headed for the not-so-private hall showers. To my relief the community bathing room was empty. (I wasn't too thrilled about disrobing this middle-aged body in front of any innocent freshmen, naïve to what twenty-five years can do to a body.) I undressed and slipped behind the curtains along the row of showers before me. I sighed with relief as the hot steamy water beat my pores with wonderfully harsh pressure.

That's when I saw it. Through the steam I could read the laminated handmade sign. "PRAY NAKED." Below those two words was a calendar. On each day of the month was a suggested person—for whom I could "pray naked": our president, a sibling, Madonna. But my eyes kept returning to the top of the poster, dripping with water droplets. PRAY NAKED. Of course. I hadn't succeeded in hiding myself after all. I can hide behind this shower curtain from the rest of the world, but I cannot hide from the One who made me and knows me better than I know myself. When I come before his throne of grace to pray, talk, or cry out to him, I am, in the truest sense, naked. I cannot hide anything from the One who sees all. I am stripped of all that I hide behind—my excuses, my sophistication, my defenses, my facades and pretenses, my rationalizations. Once stripped, my shame and embarrassment over who I am is exposed, but then I receive the rich, warm cleansing shower of his grace. How wonderful and freeing it is to know that we always "pray naked" to our Lord who sees us as we are and, with forgiving love, listens to all we say to him.

> Nothing in all creation is hidden from God's sight. Everything is uncovered and laid bare before the eyes of him to whom we must give account.
>
> HEBREWS 4:13

RGM

Unrestrained and Unrequiring

The first time I saw Kaye Lane, she was sitting cross-legged on her twin bed in the bedroom she shared with her mother. Her almond-shaped eyes, the hallmark of Down Syndrome, squinted and blinked as she sized me up. I was her nephew's new girlfriend, a seventeen-year-old neophyte in this family, and she—well, she was queen of her world.

Kaye was born in the 1940s, a time when disabled people were shrouded quietly at home or hidden away in institutions. The world was unprepared for difference, unfamiliar with tolerance. No "handicapped" parking spaces, no wheelchair ramps, no Special Olympics. For two days after Kaye was born, no one said anything to her mother about her baby. Nurses, doctors, and family members were polite but evasive when she asked to see her baby. On the third day a new nurse on shift had a quick and cutting answer to her question.

"Hasn't anyone told you? Your baby is a Mongolian idiot!"

The words struck like a shotgun blast, but in a breathless daze Ruth Lane demanded to see her daughter. As doctors kindly offered to find a "nice place" for Kaye, and well-meaning friends and family shuffled nervously, a mother's love swelled. Kaye went home with her parents, commencing to rule her kingdom on Grand Avenue, the very center of town. There would be no institution for Kaye except the institution of the family.

Kaye's world was one of hugs, kisses, laughter, and tender words. I discovered that her presence gave our family an atmosphere of unrestraint. She held back neither laughter nor tears, affection nor aversion, joy nor fear. She cried every time we sang "Happy Birthday." If she liked you, she called you by whatever name she chose, usually involving an adjective describing some part of your anatomy. (I won't mention which part of *my* anatomy impressed her most.) She knew the words to every big band hit of the 1940s, and if so disposed she would sing—but only as much of a song as she could finish in one breath. She's the only person I've ever known who asked for and received an Easter egg for Christmas every year.

Standing at Kaye's graveside I reflected upon the giving and taking that goes on in a family. As for Kaye, she was a taker. She had taken our time—time that could have been spent anywhere but nurturing one who wouldn't grow. She had taken our love—love that could have been lavished on those who meet our expectations. She had taken our attention—attention that could have been focused on the day's business.

But Kaye had also given. Besides her unconditional love, she'd given each of us something of ourselves that, apart from her, we would never have known. We learned we could be givers of unrestrained, unrequiring love. Kaye had given us a glimpse of what our unselfish selves could be.

> [Love] is not self-seeking.
>
> 1 CORINTHIANS 13:5

LMP

The Main Thing

I'm ... I'm sorry, Mom," my teenage firecracker apologized for exploding at her father and me the night before. Everything in me wanted to plunge into a hard-hitting lecture. But I knew I'd only alienate her and ruin the chances of ever seeing a repentant spirit in her again. Grace, not a lecture, was the appropriate response.

"I know you didn't mean what you said. You were just mad about not getting what you wanted." I'd forgiven her, and she knew it.

A week later it was my turn. "Bethany, I'm sorry for my harsh words. Sometimes I overstate things to get your attention, but I didn't want to hurt you like that." It was her turn to forgive, and she did.

Yesterday a teary-eyed mother sat across the restaurant booth from me, staring at the fajitas she couldn't make herself eat. "What have I done wrong? What if I handle this situation so badly my daughter ends up pregnant or a drug addict or in some gutter?" It was her version of every mother's plea: Lord, help me do it RIGHT!

But "good" motherhood isn't about doing it *right*. As parents we'll make mistakes. And some of them will be real doozies. But they don't have to ruin our kids' lives.

Perfect parenting isn't possible, nor should it be our goal. Our goal is to create an environment of grace and forgiveness. From early on, our homes can be a place where it's safe to make mistakes. Loving communication must be the air we breathe; understanding and grace are the refreshing drink we offer to each other.

I have a favorite pair of jeans I've worn so often they feel like a part of me. They've been torn and patched several times, but I find myself slipping into them again and again. Given the choice, most of us will choose the comfort of something that allows us to be ourselves, even if a little mending may be necessary afterward. Home is where we should have the freedom to be ourselves. It's where Mom, Dad, or child can blow it, be sincerely sorry, and make amends. I'm not advocating sloppy or irresponsible parenting; I'm talking about doing our best and still not being perfect.

When we focus on perfect parenting, we're usually perfectionists about our children's performance as well. The atmosphere is stiff and unforgiving. In an atmosphere of love and laughter, grace allows us to laugh at mistakes that have no eternal significance and offer our children "fresh starts" and "second chances." In such an atmosphere, family bonds are tenacious, and members feel as if together they can face the consequences of any mistake.

In parenting, "right" isn't nearly so important as relationship. It reminds me of our heavenly Father. He yearns for relationship with us, knowing full well we'll never be perfect. He knows we can't get it right as his children. How can we expect always to get it right as parents?

> Bear with each other and forgive whatever grievances you may have against one another. Forgive as the Lord forgave you. And over all these virtues put on love, which binds them all together in perfect unity.
>
> COLOSSIANS 3:13-14

RGM

Magnificent Presence

Magnificent. As I write, I'm sitting by a Tennessee mountain stream. It's well worth the six-hour drive from home to be alone with my thoughts. The rustling roar of the stream is all I hear, except for the click, click of my keyboard. A spring snow has dusted the mountaintops and weighted down the outstretched limbs of pine trees. The early morning sun dances through the trees, making shadow patterns on the ground. Its warmth causes snow pillows to relinquish their hold and scatter downward. Branches nod farewell, thanking the sun for lifting their burden. They almost seem to know this is winter's last visit as they sigh in the sun's brightness.

I'm alone in this place watching cloud shadows play tag with sunlight on the side of the mountain. Not a soul in sight—no voices, just me, creation and the Creator. I think of how it must have been for the parents of humanity in the Garden of Eden. I wonder if they awakened each morning to sounds of rustling waters and whispering breezes. The only sounds they knew were the sounds of creation. The only way they knew to live was in the presence of their Creator.

It's so easy here to think of walking with God. No horns honking, no television blaring, no schedule screaming at me to get it done! I can be still and listen for God's voice, or I can walk and feel him beside me. Magnificent! How I want to be wrapped in his presence.

But I cannot stay in this place. Monday morning is somewhere out there waiting for me. So are the demands of family life and career. When my wheels hit the highway toward home, I'm not leaving God here. He won't be sitting alone by this stream. He is present with me. But I so often choose not to be fully present with him.

When Adam and Eve made the choice to look for goodness somewhere other than in God, they chose separation, rather than presence. Their conversation with the ancient serpent must have sent him away with satisfaction, but it filled Adam and Eve with fear. Suddenly they were uncomfortable with each other. Suddenly they couldn't bear to be with God. God's question "Where are you?" must have echoed throughout the garden. The Creator of the universe had every right to ask.

We have chosen to turn that question around. We bestow upon ourselves the right to ask God, "Where are you?" But his voice echoes throughout my life. "I am here. Where are you?"

You have made known to me the path of life; you will fill me with joy in your presence, with eternal pleasures at your right hand.

PSALM 16:11

LMP

Faith Weights

My body would never be the same! Women had told me so, and a few years after having my babies, I had to admit they were right. I joined the "Y" and began the not-so-fun weight-lifting program to get my not-so-firm flab to quit wiggling. Pumping iron didn't turn out to be as much fun as it looked on TV. After weeks of sweating, grunting, and going for "the burn," my relentless trainer told me to add more weight. Painful as it was, I soon began to notice firmness where flab had been.

Building faith is a lot like building muscle. Both become stronger with use. As with weight training, repetitions of resistant force and adversity build strength of faith. I've been a believer so long, my spiritual biceps should be bulging, but the workouts in my personal training program have never been easy.

Marriage is one such faith-flexing workout. *I didn't think it would be this hard, Lord. Why does he keep hurting and disappointing me? I'll just try to change him.... Wrong again! Help, God. I gave my word I'd stay.*

Add the weight of motherhood. Though I'm confident and well-read on parenting, my child develops problems I don't know how to handle. The specialists don't know either. I'm at my wit's end! *I need you, God.*

Betrayal. My trusted friend has hurt me deeply. *What purpose could this serve? How am I to respond, God?*

My faith muscle screams, "No more!" But my Personal Trainer has an even stronger faith in mind for me. Knowing where my faith muscles are weak, he designs a training program just for me. He promises to be my "spotter," never letting the heavy weights of adversity crush me. It should come as no surprise he increases the weight even more!

My teenager rebels. Everything I do is wrong and pushes her further away. I'm on my knees, crying again. *(What are we training for, Lord—the faith Olympics?)*

My friend is dying. *I don't know why this has to happen! Can I trust you to do what is best, God?*

My adult child is making destructive choices. *I didn't realize my mother-heart could still be broken. I'm powerless, Lord.* Back to my knees.

The faith muscles are flexed with every added pound of adversity. I learn to turn to God and rely on His strength more as my faith grows stronger. What sent me into a panic years ago now sends me into prayer. Gradually I'm learning to trust, rest, and pray in the midst of crisis. Could I be noticing some firmness in that faith muscle? I think I'm getting the idea. The sign of a strong faith muscle is not how much weight is supported, but how much weight is entrusted back to the Trainer.

Consider it pure joy, my [sisters], whenever you face trials of many kinds, because you know that the testing of your faith develops perseverance. Perseverance must finish its work so that you may be mature and complete, not lacking anything.

JAMES 1:2-4

RGM

Bent Over Double

My grandfather had arthritis in his spine. He was, as they used to say, "stooped." He was bent from the waist, and no amount of effort on his part could ever make him stand straight. The bones of his spine were fused together in an arc. No medicine could cure it, no surgery could correct it, and no therapy could release it. I don't remember noticing his posture when I was a child. To me he was a strong and gentle man who loved me. That was all that mattered.

Jesus encountered a woman with the same kind of affliction one Sabbath in a synagogue. She was, according to Luke 13:11, "bent over double." This woman's affliction permeated every aspect of her life. She'd walked with her face to the ground for eighteen years. Her illness affected the way she spent her days and her contribution to her family. Even her relationships were affected. Imagine spending your days unable to look into the faces of the people you love. I wonder how many times a day she must have thought, "If only I could stand up straight...."

The encounter between this woman and Jesus took place on the Sabbath. The woman was exactly where the faithful were called to be on the Sabbath, in the synagogue. She'd learned to recognize people by their robes and sandaled feet. She could only sense the stares burning in her direction. In that culture the belief that sickness was the result of sin turned ordinary people into cold, distant judges. People with permanent illnesses lived lives of shame and disgrace.

From her cocoon of shame that day, the woman heard her name being spoken. Jesus was calling her forward. With a few words and a touch, he loosened the grip of affliction and set her free. For the first time in eighteen years, she could embrace her loved ones heart-to-heart. But before the embracing and rejoicing, she acknowledged the source of her healing. "She straightened up and praised God."

Maybe we could learn from this woman—from her Sabbath obedience, from her faith in Jesus' words, from her response of praise. Maybe. But I believe the greatest lesson from this story comes through Jesus' eyes.

When Jesus looked at the woman in this story, when he looks at you and me, he didn't then and he doesn't now see what the world sees. He didn't see a woman who deserved to live in shame. As for me, he doesn't see the pounds I need to lose, the fading youthfulness of my skin, or even my failures as a wife and mother. Neither does he see my accomplishments. Jesus doesn't need to see my business card. When Jesus looks at me, he sees my heart. When he looks at you, he sees your heart. Then from his heart, he responds.

Create in me a pure heart, O God.

PSALM 51:10

LMP

Sound Impressions

Once-in-a-lifetime experiences etch their impressions in memory for a lifetime. I'll never forget my awe upon seeing my first mountain range. Nor the unforgettable sense of smallness upon cresting a sand dune to catch my first glimpse of the ocean. Recorded forever are my baby's first cry and the joy in my husband's voice as he whispered in my ear after I gave birth. On the other hand, of all the sensations captured in my memory, the most remembered images are the not-so-note-worthy—the insignificant-but-most-often-repeated.

From childhood, the aroma of yeast rolls and Lemon Pledge tickle my memory's nose. My mind's eye will always remember the breeze playing with homemade kitchen curtains and the dancing shadows cast on the ceiling by my night-light. I'll never forget our neighbor Isabelle's musical "yoo-hoo," punctuated by the screen door slamming, or the Gentry sisters' giggling rendition of "She'll Be Comin' 'Round the Mountain" as we washed dishes after supper.

Captured forever are sound bites not only from my child-hood, but from my momhood too. The happy morning bab-blings from my baby's room as she discovered and fell in love with her own voice. My toddlers singing "This Little Light of Mine" as they play in the sandbox. The raaaaraaaaaaraaaa of Big Wheel tires racing along the sidewalk in front of our house. The laughter of a station wagon full of four-year-olds on a preschool field trip, testing their emerging sense of humor by making up silly "knock-knock" jokes. The hiccupping sobs of my child who's just been mistreated by an unfeeling adult. The ginick-ginock of my teenagers' Ping-Pong game in the basement. The wrong notes and ill-timed beat of piano practice. My teenagers' excited chatter in the backseat of the minivan as I drive them home from summer camp. The spang-spang-spang of the basketball in the driveway. My daughter asking her brother for help with her calculus homework. My son asking his sister if his hair looks good "this way."

Many of the most-remembered sounds I simply overheard. I wonder what my children have overheard. Did they hear me gossiping or telling a "little white lie" over the phone? Did they hear my late-night weeping? My on-my-knees praying through the closed bedroom door? My contented humming as I dusted the furniture?

I wonder what sounds will be etched in their memory. Will they hear my laughter shared with friends? Will they recall words of love they heard me express to their father? When they think of their childhood home, will they remember music or noise? Shouting or giggling? Advice-filled lectures or listening-filled conversations?

I suppose the most-remembered sounds will, like my memories, be the day-to-day insignificant but most-repeated ones. How many times have I moaned, "When will they listen?" They were listening, as I was, and hearing the sounds of our lives. My children, like my childhood, will never be out of earshot.

The memory of the righteous will be a blessing.

PROVERBS 10:7

RGM

Dog Day Afternoon

❀

Finally the rush was over. Two days after Christmas, mail carrier Wes Johnson was looking forward to having a normal day. But his quest for normal was short-lived when he saw the note at his station. "Wes, Chuck called in sick, and we need you to run his route today."

So much for normal, so much for catching the Packers game on TV this afternoon. So much for having his day go exactly as planned. Running both his route and Chuck's meant a long, tiring day.

His day had taken an unexpected turn, but he did have some say-so in which route he did first. Usually he did Chuck's route first, then his own. But today he wanted a taste of ordinary, so he would do his route in the morning, catch some lunch, and knock out Chuck's in the afternoon. Gray dampness punctuated the post-Christmas letdown. Traffic near the mall slowed him down, trying his patience. Why couldn't people return their gifts on a day when he had only one route?

About midafternoon on his second route, Wes rounded a corner on Hansford Place and saw something unusual. Beneath the low-hanging branches of a magnolia tree, he saw the hindquarters of a very large dog. The dog appeared to be lunging at something over and over. As he came closer he could see jeans-clad little legs underneath the lurching animal. Without a thought he jumped from his vehicle and ran toward the dog. Grabbing both collar and neck, he jerked with all his might, sending the dog airborne behind him. Then he turned toward the reapproaching animal and planted himself between the dog and his victim. The Alaskan Husky surveyed the situation and, seeming to awaken from a dazed frenzy, sauntered away.

Wes turned his attention to the terrified little boy under the magnolia tree. He was crying and bleeding from bites on his upper arms where he'd shielded his face and neck from his attacker. Neighbors, aroused by the growling and barking, mixed with screams, poured out of their houses. Wes turned the child over to their care. A hero's job done, he climbed into the seat of his mail truck and drove back into his ordinary day.

That little ten-year-old boy was my son Jeff. Every time I see the scars on his strong arms I think of the "what-ifs" of that December day. What if Wes had decided his plans for the day couldn't be interrupted? What if he'd done our route first as he usually did? What if the traffic at the mall hadn't slowed him down? What if he hadn't taken a second look at the dog under the tree? I'm thankful for every breach of ordinary that entered Wes Johnson's life that day. My son is alive and well, thanks to unwelcome interruptions in a normal, ordinary day.

Many are the plans in a man's heart, but it is the Lord's purpose that prevails.

PROVERBS 19:21

LMP

Uphill Friends

An unseasonably warm June midmorn embraced us—sunny, in the nineties, and the mercury was rising. So was the road before us—rising, that is. Linda and I had decided to jog that morning, to avoid the afternoon's intensified heat and humidity. Unfortunately, the sweltering, sticky Tennessee air couldn't be avoided this day. The heat always bothers Linda more than it does me, so we had given up jogging over a mile back, settling for an aerobic walk along the country road which wound its way through cotton fields, wooded hollers, and fencerows lined with kudzu vines. As we approached the final mile, a short but steep hill lined with wild roses and honeysuckle teased us with its bittersweet proposition. I realized I was getting ahead of Linda, so I reached back with my open sweaty hand, and she grabbed on. Relying on my strength, we trudged to the top of the hill.

The experience reminded me of a time in years past when I was the one who needed help up a hill. A friend and running partner had literally pulled me up a hill that seemed insurmountable. I was so moved by the gesture that I dubbed that date on my calendar as Help-a-Friend-up-a-Hill Day. The interesting thing about that particular hill was that I ran up it routinely, but on this particular day, I didn't have it in me to make it to the top.

Hills are a routine part of life for all of us. And sometimes a hill we routinely climb will become seemingly insurmountable. Most days I can handle my husband's intensity or my children's demands. But once in a while one or the other might become a hill I can't seem to face. That's when a friend's supportive, sweaty hand is a welcome sight. It may be in a phone call, an e-mail, or encouraging words from across the kitchen table.

Every day could be Help-a-Friend-up-a-Hill Day! All of us know someone who is facing a hill today—a hurtful marriage, a frustrating job, a child with special problems. As a friend I'm powerless to remove any hill, but I can extend my hand of encouragement. I can offer my strength, my faith perspective, my hope, and the sweat of my experience. I can, with my love and friendship, say, "Hold on. We'll go this hill together."

Some hills just call for the strength of two.

> Though one may be overpowered, two can defend themselves. A cord of three strands is not quickly broken.
>
> ECCLESIASTES 4:12

RGM

A Tale of Four Cities

Once upon a time in a faraway land there was a kingdom with four cities. The center of the kingdom was a city called Passion, a city of magnificent beauty. The sun misted the morning sky with pink radiance and set the evening horizon on fire. Clapboard houses lined cozy, tree-canopied streets. As powerfully as she radiated with beauty, the city of Passion laughed with joy and wept with pain.

The people of Passion had chosen to live deeply in their souls and fully in their hearts. They loved honestly. They shared each other's lives in celebration and in loss. Sometimes they hurt each other, but they forgave and reconciled in joy. Laughter and weeping were the music of Passion. Her gates were open to all except those living in indifference and detachment.

The deepest pain of the people of Passion was that so many of their loved ones had left. Though the gates to the city were always open, few of their loved ones would ever return. They had instead moved to the distant cities of Anesthesia, Resignation, and Amnesia.

The city of Anesthesia was almost as beautiful as Passion, but her people were unmoved by it. Neither were they moved by compassion or sorrow. To them love meant a "to do" list, and loss was just "part of life." The city of Anesthesia was neat, clean, and dealt with. Many of Anesthesia's residents used to live in Passion, but life's overwhelming unfairness created a numbness that would no longer let them hear Passion's music. Lack of pain seemed a fair substitute for the joy of Passion.

A little further from Passion was the city of Resignation. While the people of Anesthesia *felt* nothing, those who lived in

Resignation chose to *do* nothing. Her streets were overgrown with weeds and thistles. Her homes were neglected inside and out. People married "because they should," had children "because it's time" and lived passively "because you're going to die someday anyway." Expressionless faces carried out meaningless relationships. No beauty. No love. No purpose. No pain.

Furthest from Passion was the city of Amnesia, where people couldn't remember the existence of love and beauty. Amnesia was a city of people whose pain disengaged their memories and their lives, whose hearts had grown so cold that they had no memory of goodness or sorrow.

The other day I had a most unpleasant encounter with a woman from Amnesia. Her poisonous words told me she didn't remember ever feeling the pain her words inflicted. Though I often visit friends in Resignation, I never stay long. The women of Resignation have buried their dreams deeply within their hardened hearts. As for Anesthesia, I used to live there, but God has unpacked my heart and moved me to Passion. I want to live as he wants me to live. I want to live fully and in Passion.

> Yet we live on; beaten, and yet not killed; sorrowful, yet always rejoicing; poor, yet making many rich; having nothing, and yet possessing everything.
>
> 2 CORINTHIANS 6:9-10

LMP

Orange Barrels

Orange barrels. The sight of them makes my heart sink. I can be tooling along down the highway, making good time, enjoying the scenery. Then an intimidating row of those hideous orange tubs appears in the not-so-distant future.

Recently Linda and I treated ourselves to a road trip together. We were looking forward to the drive as much as any part of the trip. Sometimes half the fun is getting there. The miles were whizzing past us as we crossed the state of Arkansas, enjoying scenes of endless marshy rice fields, roadsides sprinkled with wildflowers and, in the distance, the hazy Ozark Mountains. Suddenly there they'd be, those stubby round statues in the road ahead. Orange barrels mean a serious slowdown, a crawl, or even a dead stop. They mean limited traffic flow, narrowed to a single lane or driving off the highway onto the shoulder. Orange barrels sometimes mean detours, potholes, and rough going. Orange barrels—our tax dollars at work.

Nobody likes the sight of orange barrels, as far as I know. I've seen some folks get more overheated than their engines over road delays. Tempers flare, daddies get impatient, and ordinary people become fuming maniacs at the wheel. It's hard to appreciate that we're being put through this inconvenience for a future good—an improved roadway.

I like to go places. On interstate highways and life's highways, I have a destination in mind, and I don't like to be hung up in traffic. But even on my life's highway are times of roadwork and improvements. Times when the Master Civil Engineer decides to break up the weak sections in my life and lay a stronger foundation. Orange barrels ahead. These are times when I'm barely moving forward. A health crisis, the loss of a friend, marital difficulties, a quandary with my child. My first reaction when I see any orange barrel ahead is, "Oh, no!"

The indicators of obstacles to smooth going are not a welcome sight. But these also indicate improvements underway. Life's obstacles may slow us down, but they also make us stronger, take us deeper, and have the potential to build Christ's character into our lives. The rough going teaches us to depend on the only dependable One, not ourselves. The next time I see orange barrels, whether I'm on the interstate or the highway of life, I need to recognize the improvement they promise and give thanks for their intrusion into my life.

> No discipline seems pleasant at the time, but painful. Later on, however, it produces a harvest of righteousness and peace for those who have been trained by it.
>
> HEBREWS 12:11

RGM

Back to the Drawing Board

If I had lived in Jesus' time the apostle Peter and I just might have been friends. Maybe I like Peter because he reminds me of my kids. One day he would seem on top of things—as if he'd cleaned his room, brushed his teeth, and shined his shoes. The next day he'd do or say something that let you know the previous day's performance might have been a fluke. Back to the drawing board.

Scripture records several one-on-one encounters between Jesus and Peter. In Matthew 16, Jesus asked a question about his identity. "Who do people say the Son of Man is?" The disciples answered that some said he was John the Baptist, others said Elijah, and still others thought he was a prophet. Then Jesus asked the sixty-four-thousand-dollar question. "Who do *you* say I am?"

Peter's answer flew out of his mouth. "You are the Christ, the Son of the Living God." Suddenly Peter was the clean-room, pearly-toothed, shiny-shoed boy. Jesus promised to put him in charge of things, give him power, give him his own set of keys. Peter's "fair-haired child" image didn't last long, however, probably because of his tendency to argue with the boss. When Jesus explained to his disciples about his death, Peter wouldn't hear of it. He took Jesus aside to straighten him out on the matter. But Jesus unveiled Peter's complete lack of understanding. "Get behind me, Satan! You are a stumbling block to me!" Back to the drawing board.

Peter argued with Jesus twice on the night of Jesus' arrest. The first time he didn't want Jesus to wash his feet. Peter had a better idea, but Jesus let Peter know that a foot bath at the hands of his Master was exactly what he needed. I can only imagine the expression on Jesus' face when Peter argued a second time that night. Peter proclaimed he'd lay down his life for Jesus. Jesus knew better and told Peter he would betray him, not just once, but three times that night.

I can't help but notice the relationship between Jesus and Peter. When Peter did something good, Jesus praised him and gave him identity. But he didn't stop with the present. He gave him a glimpse of his potential and his future. When Peter made a mistake Jesus would essentially say, "Here is truth, truth about you and truth about me. Watch how those truths work together."

I think of how often I've praised my sons for doing a good thing but failed to instill an identity of goodness within them. Neither did I help them link that goodness with their powerful potential for the future. As for their mistakes? Mistakes always reveal who we are in contrast to who Christ is. What if I helped my sons connect those dots every time? What if, like Jesus, I simply take them back to the drawing board?

He who began a good work in you will carry it on to completion.

PHILIPPIANS 1:6

LMP

The Call to Consistency

He's doing it again.

My husband and I invited friends to have dinner with us at our favorite restaurant. Always grateful for a reprieve from kitchen duty, I've been looking forward to this for several days. I revel in the moment as I slide into a booth across the dimly lit table from our good friends. Adult conversation. Relaxed atmosphere.

And now he's doing it again. Why is the behavior that annoys me most magnified a thousand times when we're with other people? I wonder if it annoys our friends, too. Is he even aware he's doing it? How can I let him know how annoying it is without putting him down or embarrassing him in front of our friends.

He keeps it up. It's an old pattern. I've seen it a million times. This is the person I know best in the world, the person I've committed to support and love, the person who will be lying next to me when I close my eyes tonight. But at this moment I feel only disgust.

I try to guard my tongue. I'm determined not to undermine others' respect for my husband. Inevitably, though, my disrespectful attitude rears its ugly head—in the form of sarcasm or disagreement or an edge on my words that betrays my inner warring self.

The friends sense the frigidity in my responses, the cut-with-a-knife tension in the air, and wonder what is going on. Probably they're surprised by what they see in me. Probably they think I'm cruel, distant, and difficult to live with. Now I repulse myself.

Later that night, a veil of tension divides my side of the bed from his.

"You seem distant," he observes.

No kidding! I think. I still don't want to talk, but I know we need to.

"I don't like myself right now," I tell him, reflecting the hours-long dialogue that's been going on in my head. He's confused. I quietly tell him of the battle that has gone on within me—his behavior and how it affects me, and then how my confused responses get all twisted up and become offensive in themselves.

He listens. He doesn't much like the way he is either. We vow to try to help each other. But what I really want is to have a consistent character. Not one that is affected by the behaviors around me. Not one that is altered by the way others treat me. Not one that becomes less Christlike because my husband isn't being Christlike.

I am called to be God's woman in every situation I find myself—*especially* in situations that are not very heavenly. I pray to be responsive, but unaffected, in the adverse situations of my life. As I encounter the disappointing, the disobedient, and the disgusting, I pray for a consistency of Christlike character that is unshakable, unsinkable, and immovable.

If you love those who love you, what credit is that to you? Even 'sinners' love those who love them. And if you do good to those who are good to you, what credit is that to you? Even 'sinners' do that.

LUKE 6:32-33

RGM

Generation Gap

My son Jeff and I were sitting at the kitchen table one morning when the generation gap tiptoed in and whacked me on the back of the head.

"Aw, Tiny Tim is dead," I announced as I surveyed the front page of the newspaper.

"Huh?" Jeff turned his eyes toward me with cereal milk dripping from chin to bowl.

"Tiny Tim. He's dead."

"Whoze zat?" Here came the generation gap slipping right between us.

"This guy," I said, showing him the front-page picture.

"I still don't know who he is." More gap.

"Well, he had a hit record in the sixties."

"A hit what?"

"Record, you know—song."

"Oh, yeah? What was it?"

The generation gap danced all around the room, laughing and pointing it's long, bony finger at me.

"Actually it was more than a song. It was more of an image." I was desperate.

"Some image," he said, glancing again at the front-page picture. "So what was the song anyway?"

"Tiptoe Through the Tulips," I answered quietly.

"Do what?" he asked, sure he misunderstood me.

The generation gap no longer danced; it flexed its muscles wide and long between my son and me. How could I explain someone like Tiny Tim to him? How could I explain the need of my generation to return to and express the silliness of childhood? Something was stolen from us when we learned too young the meaning of the word *assassin*. We were taught to fear invasion and nuclear attack by a generation that had known the destruction of war. In our teen years we buried our brothers, best friends, and fiancés—victims of a war we didn't understand. How could I explain to my son that Tiny Tim was an oxymoron, a combination of lost conservatism and newfound rebellion. He was a comic relief, an invitation into the absurd. Tiny Tim and all he stood for defied explanation.

There was actually no way to save the moment, so I decided to plunge feet-first into the gap. "Actually, he played a ukulele," I said, gathering my courage. "The song went like this...." Playing my best air-ukulele, I performed a rendition of Tim's claim to fame that would have made him proud. My son just stared a blank, I-can't-believe-you-just-did-that stare.

"Whatever," drip, drip.

Sometimes the generation gap is an uncrossable chasm.

Ask the former generations and find out what their fathers learned, for we were born only yesterday and know nothing, and our days on earth are but a shadow.

JOB 8:8-9

LMP

The Radical Prayer of a Radical Mother

❀

I woke up praying. "Lord, be with Bethany today." I was troubled over my teenager's bruised self-worth and how it was manifesting itself in her relationships. If she didn't resolve her vulnerability in this area, I could foresee it ruining her future.

"Keep her safe, Lord." I prayed for her over a cup of tea at my kitchen table that morning. Later I pleaded with God as I jogged through the neighborhood. "Protect her from making any huge mistakes." As I went through my day, her name was persistently lifted heavenward from my heart. "You know, Lord, if you don't fix this area of her personhood, she won't be able to have a healthy marriage or a contented life!"

That evening, as Bethany studied and talked on the phone in her bedroom, I sat on our deck and talked to the Creator of the full moon and star-studded sky overhead. "God, I don't want her to experience pain." I whispered my prayer into his presence-filled darkness.

That's when Truth interrupted. Truth challenged me to pray in accordance with what I know to be true and in agreement with God's desires. After all, God promised us we'd have whatever we ask—if we ask according to his will.

So what is the truth? The truth is that God is already with Bethany. "And surely I am with you always ..." (Matthew 28:20b). I suppose it was faithless of me to pray for something he says is already true. The truth is that God has already promised to protect Bethany. "He ... protects the way of his faithful ones" (Proverbs 2:8b). I don't have to ask him to protect her; instead I can thank him he's already doing it! But what about my prayer for her complete physical, relational, and emotional safety—in other words, my prayer that she not experience pain.

"What have I used to teach you life's most important lessons?" The question came into my mind, and I immediately knew who was asking. I answered reluctantly. *"You've used pain, Lord."* As I reflect on my life, I can see how God has used painful experiences to conform me to the image of his Son. If I asked God to prevent my daughter from hurting in life, she would perhaps miss life's richest lessons. My prayer for absolute and complete safety could actually conflict with God's perfect will for his child, my daughter.

How then is a mother to pray? I wondered. I wrestled uncomfortably with how to pray in agreement with the will of the One who loved her more than I did. *Lord, strengthen my child that she may resist the ploys of the enemy. Draw her closer to Yourself with every breath she takes. Grow her into a spiritual woman yielded and dependent on You ... whatever it takes.* I knew that was the radical will of my Father. It had become the radical will of this mother. It was a radical day in my prayer life.

I tell you the truth, my Father will give you whatever you ask in my name. Until now you have not asked for anything in my name.

JOHN 16:23-24

RGM

A Time to Dance

My mother and grandmother died while they were danc-ing. With each other. In a saloon in Chokoloskee." These beginning words drew me into a novel by Connie May Fowler and compelled me to journey through the lives and history of three strong, stubborn women. They loved, they fought, they forgave, and they danced.

I know I tread in dangerous territory when I speak of it, but dancing stands alone as a form of expression of emotion, of abandonment. I guess I qualify as an expert when it comes to watching people dance, having stood on stage as the lead singer in a rock band for ten years or so. I saw people dance who couldn't. Saw a few who probably shouldn't. Every now and then I would notice someone in a crowd who moved with fascinating fluidity. I would find myself watching that person all night long.

Real dancers dance with all of their being—movements free-ing the rhythm of the soul. They dance as though connected to something unseen, to something that waits for their dancing. They dance as though no one is watching. They dance as though they have never known sadness. They dance as though somewhere in their dance they will find themselves.

Scripture mentions mourning and dancing as opposites: "a time to mourn and a time to dance" (Ecclesiastes 3:4). When we mourn we turn our face to the ground and wonder if God is really good. When we dance we let our face shine and won-der at how good God really is. King David danced before the Lord in joyful thanksgiving. He speaks of it in Psalm 30:11-12: "You turned my wailing into dancing; you removed my sackcloth and clothed me with joy, that my heart may sing to you and not be silent."

I want a heart that sings and a soul that dances. I want to dance as though God is waiting for my dancing. I want to dance as though he alone is watching. I want to dance as though I have never known sadness. I want to dance as though somewhere in my dance I will find God's pleasure. And, like the women in the saloon, maybe I will die dancing.

David, wearing a linen ephod, danced before the Lord with all his might.

2 SAMUEL 6:14

LMP

Lonely Lolly

❀

Loneliness, loss of job, friendlessness, loss of a loved one—my friend Lolly's letter described a life of total despair. I immediately made the long-distance call to throw her a proverbial life preserver. I suggested some steps she could take to build a support system—as a kind of ladder leading out of her pit of despair. She began with the usual excuses—PMS, a busy schedule, no clothes that fit. Saddened because I couldn't nudge her out of her pity party, I promised to get together with her the following week when I would be in her town (my first visit in over a year to the city where I used to live).

Upon my arrival I called Lolly to arrange our get-together. She was having a problem with ants in the kitchen. "What else can go wrong in my life?" she cried. I tried to encourage her. I told her I'd written sample resumes and cover letters. I wanted to help her get her life back on track. When I called her later, she anticipated a hair appointment, the car needed to be washed, and junior needed new blue jeans.

"Just call me when *you* get time for me," I said.

On my final day in town, she called to let me know she was "kinda busy," since she needed to "work out." She was sorry she didn't have time to see me while I was in town.

Here was a woman in her thirties, living a lonely life without any friends. I'm sure she'll continue to feel sorry for herself and cry out to God, "Why don't you give me a friend?" She'll continue to complain that she's all alone in this world. She'll continue to whine about how nothing good ever happens in her life … just one bad thing after another.

If I had the opportunity to mentor this lonely woman, I

would teach her what I've learned about friendship. Friendship isn't determined by how much or how many people love and care about me. Rather, it's determined by how well I love and care about others. The loneliest people are those who protect their independence, prioritize their own needs, and focus on themselves—their lonely selves. Those richest in friendships focus on how they can better love, serve, and care about others.

Lolly will remain lonely as long as she's unwilling to receive the people God sends into her life. It saddens me to know she'll walk this earthly journey alone, at least as long as she refuses to make time for others and go beyond herself. Friendship at its best is an incomparable treasure, but such companionship in this life requires a priority of caring for others and a sacrificing of autonomy. It's a life principle. Give and it will be given to you.

> Greater love has no one than this, that he lay down his life for his friends.
>
> JOHN 15:13

RGM

Listen Well, Love Well

The aroma of fresh coffee drew me out of my Saturday morning sleep. When I could resist it no longer, I fumbled into the kitchen and poured myself a cup of liquid animation. My husband was in the den, fixated on TV highlights of yesterday's golf tournament, his mind buzzing with the details of his week. Efforts at conversation were pointless. My teenage boys dragged themselves to the refrigerator one at a time and grunted animal-like responses to my morning greeting. The household stupor seemed reason enough for me to head out for my Saturday morning round of grocery shopping.

An extra cup of coffee was calling my name as I passed a string of fast-food, breakfast-on-a-bun restaurants. I wheeled into the nearest drive-thru, and my first real conversation of the day began with white noise.

"May I help you?" said the garbled voice in the little black box.

"One large coffee, please."

"That's a coffee and a ham and cheese."

"No, just coffee."

"Oh, a muffin and coffee."

"No, one large coffee, that's it."

"A large coffee and a biscuit?"

"ONE—LARGE—COFFEE!!"

"Would you like cream and sugar with that?" I didn't answer.

With one hard-earned cup of coffee in hand, I headed for a close encounter with an ATM. A smiley face on the screen greeted me as I obediently inserted my card and entered my code.

"Incorrect Code. Please try again." I did. "Incorrect Code. Please try again."

"What do you mean? I know my number. Obviously you don't." I was having a conversation with a computer screen.

"Unable to Complete Transaction."

"Fine! Cut me off! Look, I have hands! I can write a check!"

Things weren't much better in the grocery store. I ran into a friend whose child kept doing a trapeze act on the cart as we tried to talk. After being waited on at the checkout by a gum-smacker who made eye contact only with my potatoes, I arrived at home frustrated. Our dog began his usual wag-and-tackle dance routine to which I responded, "Get down!" When he tucked his tail and slinked away, I realized he was the first one to listen to me all day.

My scarcity of listeners wasn't for lack of effort on my part. I had attempted to communicate with a sleep-fogged family, a talking breakfast menu, a money-grubbing computer, a distracted friend, and a bored-to-death clerk. I had been depersonalized, devalued, and ignored.

Listening is such a simple thing to do. Why is it so rarely done well? We have person-to-person contact every day. When we listen, when we make eye contact, when we "lean in," we give value to the person we're with. Listening is an authentic way of loving others. It may be the best gift you bring to a relationship. Your husband, your kids, your best friend, the convenience-store clerk—all want to be listened to. You'll have opportunities to listen all day long. Listen well.

He who answers before listening—that is his folly and his shame.

PROVERBS 18:13

LMP

Magic Carpet Ride

❁

I could hear her laughter from the next room. A warm, familiar sound. Perhaps it's this very sound that calls the grown-up me back home for visits with my parents. Caught now in this magical moment, the sound of my mother's laughter was transporting me to that other time, to recurring scenes from my childhood.

The magic carpet of my mother's laughter wrapped itself around me, becoming again my childhood security blanket. Suddenly my little-girl self was enveloped in the sound of her laughter, echoing through the house as she talked on the kitchen phone. I could always count on her laughing out loud within about ten seconds of putting the phone to her ear. From her and her mirth I learned about the joy of relationship.

She taught me to laugh over spilt milk and kitchen pots in the living room catching drips from our leaky roof. She taught me to snicker at my amateurish sewing attempts yielding uneven hems and crooked seams. And, oh, how we giggled over our verbal blunders and bungled recipes. From her lightheartedness I learned to see the humor in our humanness and imperfect circumstances. I learned the health of laughing at oneself.

On summer nights—after an evening of catching lightning bugs, playing flashlight tag, and eating too much popcorn or watermelon or homemade ice cream, I would lie exhausted in my upstairs bedroom, listening to my parents' low voices as they sat in the yard swing under the night sky. Their laughter drifted in on the night breeze through the screens of my bedroom window, and I felt loved.

I remember weekend visits to my grandparents' home and

being sent to bed long before I was sleepy. I lay there in the dark, overhearing my mother and grandmother and aunts telling stories and laughing loud and long into the night. It was the music that put me to sleep. It was the ultimate security blanket.

In my teen years my mother continued to affirm my worth by sharing the treasure of her laughter with me. Often she would wait for me to come in from a date, and together on my bed we'd share a winter cup of hot chocolate. Like two girl-friends we giggled as I debriefed her about my evening adventure, and she told me stories from her teenage escapades.

My magic carpet ride into my own past reminded me of the importance of my mother's laughter in my life. I once read that the most beautiful sound to a child is the sound of Mother's laughter. I recognize now the truth of that statement. I wonder if I've gifted my own children with enough of my laughter to weave their own magic carpet.

The Lord has done great things for us, and we are filled with joy.

PSALM 126:3

RGM

Cynthia's Cross

In the wee hours of the morning on December 2, 1995, twenty-three-year-old Cynthia was working alone, preparing the night deposit for the pizzeria where she was manager. With bank bag in hand, she locked up around 3:00 A.M. Just as she closed the door of her truck, she heard a metallic tap on her window. A disheveled-looking young man, accompanied by his girlfriend, demanded the moneybag and Cynthia's purse. She gave them what they wanted and turned to start her truck. Two shots rang out. Cynthia's life was exchanged for $1,851 in cash.

Twelve hours later with the discovery of Cynthia's body, my friends Roger and Catherine Holmes began an unthinkable journey—the journey of grieving the loss of their daughter. Excellent police work resulted in the arrest of two people within a few days of Cynthia's death. The suspects were defiant and hostile upon their arrest. Their plan to imitate the movie *Natural Born Killers* had been destroyed. The male suspect's defiance gave way within hours of his arrest, and he confessed to everything, refusing to implicate his girlfriend.

The weeks and months following Cynthia's death hung heavy with unspeakable grief for those who knew and loved Cynthia. But the family of a murder victim must deal with far more than sorrow. The cry for justice echoes through the valley of pain. It wasn't until two years later that Daniel H. was sentenced to life in prison.

In January 1998, when the trial for the female suspect was finally set, no one knew what to expect. The case against her was weak at best, but on the afternoon of the trial, a quiet, auburn-haired young woman stood before the judge and, to everyone's surprise, pleaded guilty. She was sentenced to twenty-five years and was granted her request to meet with Cynthia's parents. As they sat in a tiny room, Angie S. looked at her victim's parents and said, "I'm sorry." But there was more.

"Because of Cynthia's death, I now have life." In a solitary confinement cell, with only a Bible and the Holy Spirit, Angie met Christ. She took Catherine and Roger's hands in hers and prayed what Catherine said was the "most tender and sincere prayer I have ever heard." Deep sorrow filled Angie's words as compassion filled Catherine's heart. They wept together. They embraced. By pleading guilty, Angie had relinquished her chance for freedom, but her heart was free. The rip in Catherine's heart will never go away. But neither will it fester with bitterness nor burn with vengeance.

As she turned to leave, Catherine reached around her neck and removed a cross.

"This was Cynthia's. Would you like to have it?"

A cross once worn by Cynthia now adorns the throat of her murderer.

Somewhere in glory, three women will stand before the throne of grace. Cynthia, Catherine, and Angie—redeemed, reconciled, and set free. To God be the glory.

> Therefore, if anyone is in Christ, [she] is a new creation; the old has gone, the new has come!
>
> 2 CORINTHIANS 5:17

LMP

74

Rearview Driving

Not long ago, my husband and I were driving down a Tennessee highway—homeward bound after a long weekend trip. (The weekend wasn't long, but the trip was.) Within a half-hour of home with Mike behind the wheel, there was no question he knew where he was going and knew the road well. Suddenly I noticed the car was edging onto the paved shoulder and off the road. I hated to be a backseat driver, but two wheels off the road can be cause for alarm.

"Mike?!" was all I could get out, with panic in my voice.

He quickly jerked the wheel back onto the right lane and said defensively, "What?"—as if he hadn't noticed anything amiss.

I calmly explained, "You appeared to be going off the road."

Perhaps because of my unaccusing tone, he felt safe enough to admit what had happened. He had been distracted by something going on in his rearview mirror. While that had his attention, he lost his sense of direction.

Isn't that how it is for all of us, when our focus is on what's behind us? When our focal point is our past, we lose our sense of direction, we get off-track, and forward progress is compromised. With eyes on life's rearview mirror, we lose our sense of purpose. As a consequence we're robbed of the peace and joy of a God-centered life.

Memories can be wonderful treasures—capturing the warmest and best of life. But our memory banks are also full of disappointment, failure, and injury. If a soul is wounded deeply enough, could the memory of it hurt even more than the original injury? Remembering can inflict pain or reopen the wound left by deep loss. These painful memories easily become a focal point (like the rearview mirror) and keep us from celebrating the gifts God gives us.

Glancing in the rearview mirror can lead us to understanding, but it cannot be our guide. It's easy for me to run off the road when I'm busy looking in the rearview mirror. And when I do, I miss the joy that lies just ahead.

> But one thing I do: Forgetting what is behind and straining toward what is ahead, I press on toward the goal to win the prize for which God has called me heavenward.
>
> PHILIPPIANS 3:13-14

RGM

A Few Good Rules

I knew what he was going to say before the words came out of my husband's mouth. "Life would be a lot easier around here if you guys would just follow a few simple rules!" Rules. Every household has them. Without rules life would be chaotic, disordered, messy, and late. But just how few and how simple are our rules?

Put dirty dishes in the dishwasher, not on the counter.

Wipe your feet.

Close the door behind you.

Turn off the lights.

Make your bed.

Flush!

Don't leave your shoes in the middle of the floor.

No phone calls after 10 P.M.

No back talk.

Don't interrupt me when I'm talking on the phone.

No whining!

I could go on, but you get the point. Rules at our house seem pretty simple, but they aren't few. I tell teachers in my workshops to have a "few good rules" in their classrooms. I wonder why I haven't followed my own advice at home.

In one of my favorite scenes in the movie *Teen Wolf,* the main character, Scott, goes to his basketball coach for some advice about life. The coach tells him he lives by three rules: 1) Never get fewer than twelve hours sleep. 2) Never go out with a woman with a tattoo of a dagger on her body. 3) Never play cards with a guy who has the same name as a city. "After that," he says, "everything else is cream cheese."

Jesus lived in a time and culture of rules upon rules, especially rules about what you could and couldn't do on the Sabbath— the day of rest. You couldn't spit in the dirt because you were considered to be plowing. You couldn't walk around with one shoe on because it was assumed you were carrying the other one; carrying your shoe was considered work. You couldn't put vinegar in your mouth if you had a toothache on the Sabbath; healing was considered work. Even Jesus got in trouble for healing on the Sabbath.

No wonder someone finally asked Jesus what he thought was the best rule of all—"the bottom line," the "mother of all rules." The question was, "What is the greatest commandment?" Jesus originated the idea of a few good rules. He laid it out for them like this: 1) Love God with all of your being. 2) Love people and treat them as well as you treat yourself.

I like narrowing down the rules I need to remember. I wonder how things would go around this house if we really lived by just those two rules. Loving God would take care of attitudes, pity parties, tempers, self-indulgence, overspending, overworking, underworking, anything that takes time and honor away from God. The "people" rule would take care of everything else. Sounds simple enough. Love God. Love people. After that, everything else is cream cheese.

> Love the Lord your God with all your heart and with all your soul and with all your mind.... Love your neighbor as yourself.
>
> MATTHEW 22:37, 39

LMP

On Purpose

"M ommy! He's messing up the game—on purpose!" The last two words, elongated by an indignant whine, emphasized the culprit's motive. Little brother is not only messing up; he's doing it "on purpose!"

Some years later, I realized I was the one messing up, but it wasn't on purpose. On this particular day I was running late for everything. Breakfast Bible study with teenage girls at McDonald's. Aerobics class at the synagogue. A quick shower. A committee meeting with moms from school. Tutoring after lunch. Carpooling after school. Chauffeuring one child to a piano lesson, one to soccer practice. Pant, pant. After transporting my soccer player to play practice, I drove my pianist home to change for her volleyball game. The phone was ringing as I walked in the door; it was my husband, wanting to know what's for supper. Supper? I had the keen sense I was living a full life (at a fast pace), but I wasn't living "on purpose."

Purpose implies a plan and a commitment to priorities. Plan and priorities? It seemed I was living according to everyone else's plans, and my priority had become getting everybody where they wanted to be—somewhere close to on time. Fulfillment eluded me as I moved through my maze of demands, opportunities, and commitments. If God had any other plans for my day, I'm sure I viewed them as annoying interruptions.

As I study Jesus' life, I continually note his choices. He knew his time on earth was limited, yet his purpose-filled life looked so different from mine. No watch, no appointment book, no beeper, no cell phone. While his Father's will dictated his choices, my family's needs and demands had usurped mine. I was most startled at Jesus' choice as he responded to the life-and-death call to heal Jairus' dying daughter in Mark 5. In spite of the urgency of the little girl's need, he stopped (yes, stopped!) to ask who had touched his garment. He paused to speak with the woman who needed the peace and freedom only he could offer.

Jesus never lost sight of his purpose—not for one minute. By the end of three years he could say to his Father, "I have brought you glory on earth by completing the work you gave me to do." By investing his time, minute by minute, he successfully spent his life. As I hold up the use of my time alongside God's priorities for my life, I often see wheels spinning instead of a life of purpose.

The challenge of my life on earth is to translate my lifelong priority into my daily realities. As I plan my day, week, month or year, I check for alignment with my purpose of glorifying God. Sometimes the urgent will have to wait, the complicated will have to be simplified, and the must-dos will have to go undone. If I'm to fulfill my purpose, I must learn to live life "on purpose."

He has showed you, O [woman], what is good. And what does the Lord require of you? To act justly and to love mercy and to walk humbly with your God.

MICAH 6:8

RGM

Bent Tree

"Just a little more!" Bekah was directing Mike as he straightened the little tree to an upright position. The dogwood in their front yard was the victim of the most recent West Tennessee ice storm. Under the weight of the ice, it bowed at the waist, sweeping the ground with the tips of its branches. We tied twine around it, yanked it to an obedient stance, and staked it. As an extra precaution we tied it to a nearby oak. We figured that a couple of months in traction should have the little guy standing at attention.

When spring arrived, Bekah and I went outside for the official restraint removal. She pulled up the stake and let the twine go loose. So far so good. I cut the lifeline to the oak and—THWAK! Down it went, just as penitent-looking as it was before twine and stakes. Maybe we couldn't do anything to straighten this little one out. Maybe we were stuck with a bent tree.

That little bent tree and I are what you might call kindred spirits. Proverbs 22:6 says, "Train up a child in the way [she] should go, and when [she] is old [she] will not depart from it." The phrase "way [she] should go" can be translated, "as she is bent." Children all have a "bent." I admit that mine was a miserable disappointment to my mother.

My mother is a home economist by profession, with all the domestic skills that go with it. I, on the other hand, was born with a baseball in my right hand and a cap pistol in my left. It didn't help that a girl hadn't been born in the McNatt family in thirty-six years. I had an older brother, and all of my older cousins were boys. Mom tried to dress me in pinafores when I was little; I would come out of Sunday school with both straps hanging around my waist. She gave me dolls to play with, but they ended up stuffed under my bed. Mom even tried to teach me to sew when I was about twelve—sort of a last-ditch effort toward femininity. That didn't work either.

Knowing your child well will help you know their bent. If you're training your son or daughter in a way other than their bent, they'll just snap right back into place as soon as you pull up the stakes. My mom surrendered the idea of having a daughter who would wear ruffles and help her make curtains. But she did encourage me to write for the school newspaper when I was in high school, a bent that has gradually given direction to my life. I don't plan to depart from it.

Know your children well. Know their bent. Help them grow into the men and women God created them to be—no twine and stakes needed.

Train a child in the way he should go, and when he is old he will not turn from it.

PROVERBS 22:6

LMP

You Don't Trust Me

Y ou don't trust me!"

My teenage daughter was screaming at me again. How many times had we had this "conversation"?

The truth was, I didn't trust her. She had destroyed all trust a year earlier when I discovered she'd been lying to me. I was slow to believe my own child could look me in the eye and tell me a bold-faced lie. (I could never have lied to my mother, I reasoned.) Honesty was a value we had taught our children from the very beginning. Her lying just seemed an impossibility.

I was naïve. Her strong will went into overdrive. Her desire to be with her peers, her desire to do what her peers were doing, and, perhaps most important, her desire to gain her peers' approval—all overshadowed her sense of integrity and desire for parental approval. Her internal battles between these competing desires must have been agonizing, but she made her choice. The peer group didn't win; a different enemy did. This enemy reveled in rebellion and deceit. This enemy wanted to drive a wedge between mother and daughter that could destroy our relationship. And this enemy seemed to be winning.

She said she was going someplace, but later I heard she was seen someplace else. She promised to be home by nine o'clock, but at ten she came in saying her watch was malfunctioning. She claimed she had a banana for breakfast, but no banana peeling could be found. Individually, instances such as these seemed insignificant (and, believe me, she tried to convince me they were), but together they were a smokescreen for a darkness that was taking over her life.

I had to do something, but I knew radical restraint would

provoke and anger the spirit of this strong-willed child, probably resulting in her leaving our home. It was a terrifying time, steeped in prayer. No parenting classes had prepared me for this, and I feared crossing a line that would forever separate my life from my daughter's.

I continued to give her choices, but choices she could not easily abuse, choices that would not endanger her. While she might be permitted to spend time with the friend who was not a good influence, it had to be on our turf. She could go to the mall, but it would be with me. She could spend the night at a friend's, but I would talk to the parent first and later call to make sure my daughter was where she said she was. "You don't trust me!" I heard it many times over the next few years.

That's right, my child. I don't trust you. I love you and want to trust you, but you have undone my trust. You will now have to rebuild my trust by your own trustworthiness. And it will take time for you to prove you are truly trustworthy. Forgiveness is given, but trust is earned.

Whoever can be trusted with very little can also be trusted with much, and whoever is dishonest with very little will also be dishonest with much.

LUKE 16:10

RGM

Holy Desperation

❀

People do strange and out-of-character things when faced with a desperate situation. Men of integrity become thieves to feed a starving family. People who have never spoken the name of God become people of prayer when walking the line between life and death. Ordinary people become heroes when the moment's salvation depends solely on their response. But in the lives of mothers, desperation is not limited to situations; it seems to be a permanent guest in our souls.

Desperation enters our lives almost as soon as we discover that the life within depends completely upon our choices for food, drink, exercise, and rest. I don't know that it ever leaves us. I remember when my father-in-law had open-heart surgery about twenty years ago. On the faces of those sitting in the waiting room that day I could see worry, fear, compassion, and hope. But only one countenance, that of his eighty-something-year-old mother, showed desperation.

Crisis isn't necessary to awaken desperation in my heart. I feel it every Friday night when my son the quarterback faces off with a wall of flesh whose single purpose is to bring him down. I sense it every time my older son hops in his Jeep and wheels out of the driveway. Desperation visits me because I cannot, or should not, protect them from all of life's dangers and hurts. I'm desperate for their good, their growth, and their safety. I long to know them better and love them more deeply as they grow and change.

Rarely do we think of God as a parent acquainted with desperation. We worship his power, his might, his holiness, and his love, but how deeply he lives in his longing for his children. We hear his desperation as he calls out to Adam in the garden, "Where are you?" We see it as he tenderly makes clothing to cover his rebellious children. We follow his relentless pursuit of the children of Israel and hear his continuous plea, "Return to me." We see desperation in the eyes of Jesus as he calls the sick, the lame, and even the sinner out of the crowd. We hear it in his voice as he asks Peter, "Do you love me?" God is desperate for his children.

Sharon Hersh insightfully says, "Seeing God's desperation can transform mine."* Desperation motivated by deep, godly love is holy desperation. When I find myself surrounded and pursued by the love of a desperate God, then my mother-desperation is no longer a nail-gnawing, at-my-wit's-end, gotta-have-it-just-so desperation. Desperation, couched in trust of a loving, pursuing God, is transformed into a tender longing. One that only a mother's heart can know.

> I have no greater joy than to hear that my children are walking in the truth.
>
> 3 JOHN 4

LMP

---

*"The Desperation of God," *Mars Hill Review,* Fall 1997, 19–29.

Family Feud

Family squabbles are natural, I guess. But this was my church family—a family supposedly sold out to doing what pleases God. Unified in purpose, shouldn't we all want the same thing? I guess I was naïve and had some growing up to do.

I accepted an enormous ministry responsibility that year. I felt equal to the task, strapped on my spiritual tool belt, and got down to business. Months in advance I recruited and trained a crew of workers, designed a mission statement, strategized, prepared, and prayed. I was excited to be part of this best-ever ministry endeavor—until someone in leadership started raising their eyebrows.

"What's the problem?" I probed, hoping to deal with any difficulties head-on, openly, and honestly.

No one would actually tell me what the "problem" was, but there was definitely a hitch, a snag, a no-way-around-it roadblock. It was like driving seventy miles per hour on your way to a rendezvous with your best friend and finding the road blocked with a great big sign: "You can't get there from here!" Screeeeeeeech!

With smoking tread marks in my rearview mirror, I stewed for three months about what to do, as if I had a choice. Actually, the choice was in choosing my own attitude toward this seemingly un-Christlike handling of the situation. I could submit graciously to the ministry leader. Or I could submit bitterly and grudgingly, making sure others knew how I'd been hurt. But, as I envisioned the discord I could sow, I felt God's heartache. The voice of self-preservation within me screamed, "Just quit!

Walk away!" Yet I knew the legacy I would leave behind would be as a woman who didn't get her way so she left.

I didn't just stew about it. I prayed ... and prayed ... and prayed. It wasn't that difficult to figure out what obedience looked like. But it would require the difficult relinquishment of my will, my agenda, my idea about how to minister best. I knew God wanted me to act and think with grace—regardless of how I was treated, regardless of decisions based in narrowness or shortsightedness, regardless of the "rightness" or "wrongness" of the situation.

God used this hurtful experience to teach and grow me. At first I thought the enemy was my fellow church member. But in reality the enemy was the one who tempted me to be bitter and resentful. The one who justified unforgiveness and revenge. The one who would rejoice over discord in the bride of Christ and my withdrawal from my church family.

Along with my Father, the grace-giver, I'm pleased to announce that the enemy didn't win. And if any "family squabbles" are in my future, I feel sure I won't take so long in choosing grace and patience with my brothers and sisters in Christ. In the long run, even in the eternal realm, it will be our gracious character, not our ministry successes, that will be remembered.

Be completely humble and gentle; be patient, bearing with one another in love.

EPHESIANS 4:2

RGM

Soul Music

On Mother's Day morning, our Sunday school teacher asked us to take a moment to reflect and to celebrate our mothers. We were given an opportunity to share moments remembered and lessons learned. The responses were as diverse as the microcosm of society seated in our classroom each Sunday. Some were tearful, some were funny, but all were honest tributes to the women who gave life and then gave their lives to their children.

Memories of my mother take me back to a knotty pine kitchen with slick, chrome-trimmed countertops. The aroma of corn bread hints that dinner is almost ready. The music of my mother's humming floats around the room, trailing behind her like a kite tail. The room resonates with "cooking sounds"—simmering, sizzling, spoons clicking—and with humming. Our little family of four dines like royalty; we taste the music of my mother's soul.

My mother's humming was a wordless parable in my life—a never-ending message proclaiming "all is well." She must have hummed to me when I was a baby. She must have hummed as she changed my diapers, heated my bottles, and wiped my tears. The soothing power of my mother's close-lipped melody has always hinted of connection to my beginning. But a few years ago I learned in a most unexpected way that my mother's humming must surely have accompanied those unremembered years.

The revelation came when my grandmother spent the last year of her life in my mother's home. My grandmother was ill, her condition deteriorating bit by bit as the months went by.

My mom nurtured with tender guidance when confusion clouded my grandmother's thoughts. She patiently taught and re-taught when my grandmother would forget what she was supposed to do with a fork or a toothbrush. She listened reassuringly as my grandmother melded decades into yesterday and tomorrow. Mom sacrificed her carefree days of retirement to protect my grandmother's safety and dignity.

My mom slept little, loved much—not so different from the first years of motherhood. Through it all, she accompanied her days with a gentle, reassuring melody. During my grandmother's illness I came to understand better the mother and the mothering that precede my memory. I saw the sacrifice, the nurturing, and the loving I know were given to me as I was acquainting myself with the world. I heard the tender background music—the accompaniment of my life.

My memory of my mom was unspoken that Mother's Day morning. It seemed more fitting to honor her in silence, to listen deep within myself to hear the music of my mother's soul.

Is anyone happy? Let him sing songs of praise.

JAMES 5:13b

LMP

Devil Grass

As a Midwesterner transplanted into southern California for a while, I marveled at fragrant ocean breezes, the flowered roadsides, the endless seasons of sunshine ... and year-round yard maintenance. Every Saturday morning, I determinedly faced my weekly duty of extracting unwelcome grass from my flowerbeds. Kneeling among the hardy, brilliant orange and gold gazania blossoms, I wrestled with the strangling runners growing from a network of roots—roots that ignored brick edging, plastic barriers, and even the concrete sidewalk. Within days feisty tentacles would creep in from the underside, choking my gazanias. I soon realized why the Californians called it "devil grass." As I tugged and pulled on the stubborn runners, I imagined I was at war with an enemy!

How the devil grass is like the lies that creep into my life. They approach from somewhere deep and unnoticeable. So often lies take their root in childhood and build their root system throughout our lives. Even though we think we've rid ourselves of them, they keep coming back. These lies take hold anywhere they can find some unplanted soil and choke out what is good and true.

Perhaps you've dealt with similar devil grass in your life. Sometimes it goes unnoticed, growing in your own personal garden, until it has already destroyed the beautiful blossoms of your life. Lies steal into our thinking and wreak havoc in the garden of our joy and peace, but with practice we can recognize them.

The lies of the enemy are pretty universal, with a few personalized variations. Generally falling into categories of accusations, temptations, or deceptions, the voices I hear sound something like this:

"Sure, that's a good thing to do, but you're too busy today."

"You're not good enough, smart enough, thin enough...."

"You call yourself a Christian? Look how you've failed."

"Why can't you be more like her?"

"Why don't you just give up and quit trying!"

"You deserve better! It's time to walk out!"

"It *feels* so right; it must be God's will."

"Nobody loves me."

"I don't matter."

"It's all my fault."

Heard any of these lately? One at a time, our lies subtly steal their way in between the places of growth and beauty in our lives, winding their shoots around our thoughts, self-concept, and motives until they gain a stranglehold. How often I must remind myself to recognize them for what they are—lies! How often I must remember their source—the enemy of truth!

If my garden isn't thriving with truth, the persistent lies will keep creeping in to sow discouragement, a distorted self-view, denial, or overconfidence. At the first sign of any of these I must examine the source of my thinking. If it doesn't sound like God's truth, I must yank out the intruding devil grass. So how does your garden grow, my friend?

Put on the full armor of God so that you can take your stand against the devil's schemes.

EPHESIANS 6:11

RGM

Truth Trainer

"Driver in Training," read the sign on the car door. I knew right away I should steer clear of this wavering vehicle in the next lane. I gave him lots of room as he swung a wide left to make a right turn. I expect a little "training" took place in the front seat after that one.

We have a relatively new driver at our house. My seventeen-year-old has his driver's license, a piece of plastic certifying he's considered mature enough, wise enough, and skilled enough to maneuver two tons of metal down our public streets. According to the state of Tennessee, he has had sufficient training to do so. I wonder.

The "Driver in Training" sign on the modest automobile to my right had an interesting effect on my perspective. I knew to interact with this vehicle carefully, to assume it might make mistakes or sudden changes of direction. It might stop abruptly or veer into my lane. I also knew, thankfully, that seated beside the driver was a teacher—someone who could make critical decisions in an emergency.

I wonder what would happen if our children each wore a sign: "Human Being in Training." Would our perspective and expectations be different? Would we take greater care in our interactions with them? Would we worry less and train more?

Proverbs 22:6 tells us to "train up a child in the way he should go." Training means to teach, to initiate learning. I'm a teacher by profession, by choice, and by heritage. It's my calling in life, but God has given me a much deeper calling, to teach right here in my own home. Deuteronomy 11:18-19 explains our calling: "Fix these words of mine on your hearts and minds.

Teach them to your children, talking about them when you sit at home and when you walk along the road, when you lie down and when you get up." God is clearly calling me to teach my children about him.

For my life, those words in Deuteronomy say this, "Mothers, know my word. Know it well. Know my word with your mind and remember what it says. Know my words with your heart and understand what they mean. Then teach what you know to your children at every opportunity. Teach them when you are at home. Teach them when you're driving to ballet lessons or soccer practice. Lie down with your children at night and read them stories about me, stories that teach them truth. Remind them every morning to honor me with their day."

Teaching our children truth should be as much a part of our day as driving the car or sitting down to a meal. William Barclay said, "Truth is what makes a person think and act like God." As moms, maybe we should wear a sign: "Truth Trainer." It is, after all, our calling in life.

Teach [my words] to your children.

DEUTERONOMY 11:19

LMP

Loving Proof

❀

Another birthday had come and gone. No card. No present. Like many wives I have a husband who doesn't have the gift of gift-giving. I can't say I've never received any gifts from him. I remember the waffle iron he gave me for our second anniversary. And there were those golf lessons he gave me for one birthday—wrapped in hopes that my taking up the sport would facilitate his playing more golf. But who's keeping score?

Actually most of us are keeping score. We may consider ourselves mature, selfless, and gracious, but we remember each profound disappointment. If you talk to a woman after a giftless birthday or Mother's Day or anniversary, she'll probably mention it ... and hold it in her memory for years after the fact. Gifts mean more to us than we admit even to ourselves. While the gifts may be absent on special occasions, the secret to contentment with our lives lies in noticing other gifts.

My husband's gifts come in all different forms. Picking up some milk on the way home from work. Playing with the kids. Giving me the night off from cooking and taking the family out. Folding a load of laundry I can't seem to find time for. Being a man of integrity, whose word can be trusted. Trusting me with the checkbook. Encouraging me to buy something for myself. Helping with household tasks. Telling me he loves me and is proud of me.

My father is clueless when it comes to shopping for a present for my mother. Recently she had a birthday and was mentioning to me how difficult gift-buying was for him. I reminded her that the vacuum tracks in the freshly vacuumed carpet were loving proof of his heart dedication to her. He had done the vacuuming without her even asking.

Other husbands give different gifts. Often we miss them. Have you noticed any gifts coming your way today? Some women have to look harder than others to discover the gifts in their lives. I've known some determined-to-be-grateful hearts who can come up with nothing better than this: "My husband doesn't cheat on me." "My husband doesn't beat me."

What if no gifts are coming from anyone? Don't we all need to eliminate earthly expectations? Ultimately we must turn to the perfect Giver of gifts. And it is from him we must receive, in him we must focus. When we take our eyes off him, it becomes difficult to nurture a grateful heart.

The secret to contentment may lie in recognizing the gifts, but the secret to a grateful heart lies in recognizing the Giver. His loving proof is all around us.

Every good and perfect gift is from above, coming down from the Father of the heavenly lights, who does not change like shifting shadows.

JAMES 1:17

RGM

Unexpected, but Worth Pondering

A gentle smile had taken permanent residence on Mary's young face. She just couldn't seem to make it go away. People who saw her couldn't help but return it. Neither could Mary seem to dissolve the knot of excitement stirring inside her whenever she thought about her future. Within a year she would be married to the kind of man she'd always dreamed of marrying. Joseph was a carpenter, a highly respected man, a righteous man. Life was offering Mary the fulfillment she hoped for. Her life promised to be simple, ordinary, happy, and good.

So it seemed until Mary's life was touched by an angel. The angel, Gabriel, brought a divine disruption to Mary's plan. He announced that she would be the mother of the Messiah, the Son of God, the Christ. Mary would know the magnificent terror of motherhood as no woman on earth had ever known it. She was called upon to love, nurture, cuddle, train, and release the One who would become the salvation of the world. The life she had expected would forever be out of her grasp. Her future would hold immeasurable joy and unthinkable heartache. She would later be told by Simeon in the temple that a "sword would pierce her soul."

Never would Mary have dreamed of being called "blessed among women." Never would she have imagined that Joseph would have considered breaking their engagement. Never would she have dreamed that her son, the Savior, would be born in a stable and cradled by a manger. Suddenly and unexpectedly Mary was connected to the story of God's redemption.

Mary's life had taken an unexpected right turn. She found

herself visiting her cousin instead of planning her wedding. Sewing maternity clothes instead of a wedding dress. Walking the streets through a gauntlet of whispers instead of a receiving line of smiles. For the first of many times in her life, Mary was in a hard place. The course of her life was totally unexpected— but clearly worth pondering.

We see that Mary's response of obedience to God's call springs from the deepest part of her. "My soul magnifies the Lord. And my spirit has rejoiced in God my Savior" (Luke 1:46-47, NKJV).

Later, after the birth of Jesus and the surprise visit from a group of shepherds, we learn something more of the quietness of Mary's soul. The Gospel of Luke tells us that Mary "kept these things and pondered them in her heart." Over and over, Mary revisited the places in her heart that had been touched by the finger of God. Every unexpected turn, every promise fulfilled, every whisper of divine direction, every miraculous encounter. Mary kept them all tucked away like a favored blanket, wrapping herself in their warmth, only to be awakened by their frazzled edges. Mary's life, like yours and mine— unexpected, but worth pondering.

Blessed is she who has believed that what the Lord has said to her will be accomplished!

LUKE 1:45

LMP

Traveling Mercies

"OK, everybody in the car! Have we got everything?"

"Why are you taking *that?*"

"Mommy, I forgot 'Grape Ape'!"

"Did everybody go to the bathroom?"

Ah, family vacation time. Frazzled from packing the car and "discussing" the cargo, Mike and I are not in a praying mood, so we ask for a backseat volunteer to pray for our family. Knowing the routine, one of the kids sensitively complies in asking the God of the universe to bestow upon our little troupe what is known as "traveling mercies" in contemporary Christianese. As I recall, it was some version of "Dear God, help us have a safe trip—no accident, no car trouble, good weather, and a good time for all."

In the calm following the stormy departure, I pondered our prayer. What if God wanted us to demonstrate his love to an auto mechanic or tow-truck driver? That would require a flat tire or car trouble, wouldn't it? What if we were to model patience and joy in spite of rainy days at the beach? What if my gracious survival from a car crash was part of God's plan for bringing more people into his kingdom? What if Jesus had prayed for safety in the Garden of Gethsemane—the night before his execution? With such traveling mercies, he wouldn't have gone to the cross.

Psalm 91 promises sheltering wings and protection from stubbed toes, so why do Christians experience pain, disease, car accidents, and broken bones? In Jesus' Sermon on the Mount, he promised we'd be better off than birds, lilies, and Solomon, so why are some of God's people so miserable? From what I know about my Father and his Son, such claims weren't idle pie-in-the-sky encouragement, just to ease my anxious mind. When a promise comes to earth from heaven, you can count on it. But it's not always easily understood.

If God says he's sending angels earthward to keep our feet from bruising, he means it. Yet his own Son endured beatings, torture, and a long, excruciating death. He must have meant something other than the physical safety we want to believe he's guaranteed. What kind of safety did Jesus experience as he suffered painfully on the cross? Rather than physical safety, he was secure in his Father's loving grasp and in the center of God's good and perfect plan.

What is God's idea of safety for my life, my journey, my vacation? He desires that I remain safe in the heart of his will—safe from the devil's attempts to trip me up and snatch me from my Father's grasp. The enemy would delight in a vacation ruined by hot tempers, selfishness, bad attitudes, and shameful behavior. Yes, I need to pray for traveling mercies—the kind that will keep my heart pure and undivided.

On this journey, this adventure of my life, Lord, keep my heart safe, no matter what troubles lie in the road ahead.

My prayer is not that you take them out of the world but that you protect them from the evil one.

JOHN 17:15

RGM

Saving Sons, Saving Moms

I watched the movie *Saving Private Ryan* last night with my fifteen-year-old son. Michael had seen the movie in the theater. His assurance to protect me from scenes I might not want to see made me decide to go ahead and rent a movie I knew would leave me uneasy. In reality it didn't leave me at all.

As I write this morning, after a night's sleep, I am still engulfed by what I saw, heard, and felt as I watched. To be sure, *Saving Private Ryan* is a movie about war, about death, about men who become something other than men in a place where no man should ever have to be. But it is also about moms. We are never to forget throughout the movie that Private Ryan is being sought for one reason and one reason only. Because he has a grief-stricken mother at home who is as much a victim of war as any man whose riddled, maimed body lay still on the battlefield.

And so I watched as men lay dying, crying out for the one who had always brought them consolation. "Mama! Mama!" they cried. I listened as the eight soldiers assigned to find Private Ryan tried to reason why Ryan's mother was favored above their own, his life more valued than theirs. I understood, for the first time ever, why my uncles would not speak of wartimes, not to their wives, not to their children, and especially not to their mothers. Last night I was an intruder. I was in a place not meant for the mother of any son.

As the reality of what took place some fifty years ago played out before me in bloody reds and olive drabs, my son sat by my side on the couch in our living room. When action would give way to dialogue, soldiers would speak of home and hammocks and brother-pranks. Michael played tug-of-war with his dog, snacked on chips and soda, affectionately squeezed my foot as he walked past me on his way to answer the phone. "Mom, don't watch this part," he would say as the battle scenes returned. I watched anyway. I saw it all.

I am not Mrs. Ryan. I am her granddaughter, her daughter, her sister, and her friend, but I am not Mrs. Ryan. Her telegrams came fifty years ago just as they came from Korea forty years ago, Viet Nam thirty years ago, Cuba, Panama, Iraq, Serbia....

Michael knew exactly why I held him extra long as I told him good night. I wished, just for tonight, that his room was right next door as it was when he was little. I wished I could say good night to his brother who is away for the week. I wished no mother's son would ever have to fall on the battlefield. My wishing comes as American bombs fall. God, save us from who we have become, for I am ... Mrs. Ryan.

Where, O death, is your victory? Where, O death, is your sting?

1 CORINTHIANS 15:55

LMP

The View From Down Here

S ummer trips to Granma's house were like a visit to heaven for me as a child. My sisters and I would establish a fort under the trumpet vines or play hide-and-seek between the sheets drying on the clothesline. We'd fetch tools from the shed to help Granpa in the garden, or we'd help Granma with the canning or jelly-making. Even the teasing and rough-housing of my uncle Chris brought me delight. He liked to sweep me off my feet, flip me over, and hold me upside down from my ankles. From this vantage point, life was inverted and peculiar, yet real. It was a vantage point usually afforded only a child.

I remember another interesting vantage point I discovered, though this one was in my adult years. I was rocking along in life, active in church and thinking I was living a life pleasing to God. Through fresh exposure to his Word and women of faith, God swept me off my feet and flipped me upside down. He showed me I hadn't submitted every area of my life to him. One night I knelt by my living room couch and told God I wanted him to reign in *every* area of my life—my thoughts, my conver-sation, my choices.... Within days I noticed I was seeing reality from a different vantage point.

As television programs aired immoral lifestyles and entice-ments to be self-indulgent, I became convinced I shouldn't be filling my mind with things that contradict God's ways and wis-dom. News broadcasts of horror stories about crime, hunger, and catastrophe became more than facts; they broke my heart.

When my two-year-old disobeyed, I suddenly perceived not only a defiant toddler, but the potential for a rebellious lifestyle—defying any form of authority. I felt like Super Mom with X-ray vision! Suddenly I could see beyond the face value of reality. Where did this come from?

I realized the woman who shunned me at the grocery store was hurting—not intentionally striking out at me. The woman who sang her own praises at lunch merely needed affirmation. The angry mom who screamed at the nursery worker was simply tired and needed encouragement. Suddenly I could see clearly that my child's misbehavior was a plea for boundaries as confirmation of my love.

I began listening to music that edified and encouraged me, for I was hearing with new attentiveness. When I read the Bible and other books, my mind received the words with a new understanding. Whenever God or his Word was mocked, I felt an inward grief. It occurred to me what all this must mean.

God was granting me a new vantage point as I asked him to live and rule in every crevice of my life. He was letting me see what he saw. It was a vantage point only afforded God's yielded child.

I will give you a new heart and put a new spirit in you; I will remove from you your heart of stone and give you a heart of flesh.

EZEKIEL 36:26

RGM

Poor in Spirit

I never talked to Charlotte very much. No one did, except for her one and only friend, Linda. I used to hear Charlotte whisper my name across two rows in my second-grade class. Relief poured over me when the other Linda would answer. Charlotte couldn't help the way she was. She wore the same two dresses to school most of the year. Her stringy, dark hair hung in oily clumps around her shoulders. A grayish film clung to her skin. I found out years later that Charlotte's mother washed her five children from the same basin, with the same water, starting from the youngest to the oldest. Charlotte was the oldest. The other four were boys.

My mother explained to me that Charlotte was poor. I knew Charlotte paid for her lunch every day with a ticket rather than money. I knew my mother bought an extra tablet when she bought one for me. The extra went to Charlotte. At Christmas our teacher slipped two gifts under the tree. One was tagged "to Charlotte"; the other, "from Charlotte."

Charlotte was my first encounter with poverty. Even now my mental picture for the word *poor* is Charlotte. Poverty is need, dependency, and even isolation. Jesus laced the word *poor* into an unexpected phrase in the Sermon on the Mount. He said, "Blessed are the poor in spirit, for theirs is the kingdom of heaven." The word translated "poor" has an even deeper meaning. It means helplessly poor, so poor you can earn bread only by begging. Even Charlotte was a step up from that kind of poverty. But Jesus said if you know that depth of need in your spirit, you are blessed.

Jesus brings his picture of poverty of spirit into clearer focus in the parable of the Pharisee and the tax collector. He told of two men going to the temple to pray—one a religious leader, a Pharisee; the other a tax collector, the lowest of all sinners. In his prayer the Pharisee gives God a verbal resumé concerning his prayer life and his church contributions. He makes sure God is aware of his goodness. The Pharisee had a serious case of "wealth of spirit." The tax collector, on the other hand, was so humbled by God's presence that he couldn't even look up. He could only beat his breast and beg for mercy. The tax collector was poor in spirit. Jesus honored such depth of need.

Often we see that expectation springs from wealth, but humility springs from poverty. The tax collector, like Charlotte, could only depend upon someone else to take care of his needs. Only when we understand our desperate need of God does blessedness rest upon us.

Blessed are the poor in spirit, for theirs is the kingdom of heaven.

MATTHEW 5:3

LMP

An Envelope for Him

As the server presented our bill for lunch, Lisa retrieved a plain white envelope from her purse. "Dining Out" was handwritten across the front. Recognizing the tried-and-true envelope system, I knew I'd had the privilege of eating lunch with a self-disciplined young woman. I was honored she'd used her limited funds in part to share a meal with me.

My husband's parents used the envelope system when they were newlyweds and Mully's weekly paycheck was eighteen dollars. Four dollars went into the Rent envelope, toward the sixteen dollars a month it cost to live above the feed store. Two dollars and fifty cents went into the Car Payment envelope. Separate envelopes labeled Food, Gas, Utilities, and Entertainment consumed the weekly paycheck. Mully and his bride insist they never were wanting.

Those were the days of ninety-cent light bills and forty-cent water bills—when a nickel bought a loaf of bread or a pork chop. But the envelope system works in any age or income level.

From the time our kids began making a weekly allowance of a dollar, we taught them the envelope system. Each child had an envelope for each of several categories, including Giving, Savings, and Spending. As they became teenagers with increased responsibilities and allowances, the Spending category became several envelopes—Clothing, Entertainment, Health and Beauty Aids, and Dining Out. Except when it came to Savings and Giving, they had the freedom to choose the percentage for each envelope, as well as the freedom to move money between envelopes. We set up a guideline for percentage giving and saving. Money in either of those two envelopes couldn't be removed except to be taken to the bank or given to God's work. With this system our children learned to manage limited funds, plan thriftily, spend only what they could afford on any given category, and enjoy the fruit of giving and saving.

Bethany supported a young girl in Guatemala through World Vision, and Ben supported a boy in Zaire through Compassion International. They bought their own clothes, movie tickets, fast food, stereo equipment, and first cars. What a relief to send them out into the world equipped to handle whatever resources they had!

I wonder if I'm as equipped to manage my own personal resources. If I put my living of life into envelopes, how would they be labeled? Family, Church Responsibilities, Volunteer Work. Supporting Neighbors and Friends, Recreation, and one labeled "Just for Me." This would be for things I treat myself to—like reading a good book or having lunch with a friend. The envelopes are adding up—Housework, Decorating, Gift-Giving. No wonder my life is so difficult to manage! Now where did I put that other envelope? In the midst of the pulls on my life, may I not forget that God wants an envelope of my time. And ultimately may every envelope of my life fit into one giant package with a gift tag labeled "For God."

[Her] master replied, "Well done, good and faithful servant! You have been faithful with a few things; I will put you in charge of many things. Come and share your master's happiness!"

MATTHEW 25:21

RGM

The Summer of My Contentment

❊

Summertime for me, a schoolteacher, is far more than just time away from work. It's a time when life usually loosens its vise grip, when I enjoy some say-so in how I spend my time. It's a time when my second cup of coffee can go down slowly instead of trickling down my shirt on the way out the door. Summer means breathing room for reflection, and reflection never leaves me unchanged.

Early this summer I remember sitting propped up in my bed caressing that cherished second cup of coffee. The weight of one of the most difficult school years of my career finally seemed to have lifted. My husband and my son Jeff were away on a golf trip for ten days, leaving Michael, my low-maintenance child, and me alone in a quiet, unscheduled world. I remember wondering what God had in store for me this summer. Little did I know that God was about to reacquaint me with someone I hadn't seen in a while—me.

Maybe you've had the experience of being caught up in a shoulder-to-shoulder crowd and found yourself mindlessly moving toward some unknown destination. You don't have to think about where you're going; you just end up somewhere that someone wanted you to be. Life had sort of been shuffling me forward for a couple of years. I had been consumed by writing my first book and building a house and by students with deeper problems than I'd ever faced. My life seemed to be controlling me instead of me experiencing life.

But on this particular summer morning God took his hammer and chisel to my heart as my eyes fell on 1 Thessalonians 5:23: "May God himself, the God of peace, sanctify you through and through. May your whole spirit, soul, and body be kept blameless...." My soul took the longest, deepest breath it had taken in two years. Peace? Whole? I suddenly realized how disconnected I'd become from the deepest, truest part of me.

Later that day as Bekah and I went for a long walk, I asked her to pray that verse for me. I adopted it as my theme verse for the summer. I read, studied, and prayed. I listened to my world, tasted my life, and felt my pain. I began, for the first time in a long time, to live in my heart.

At summer's end I found myself harboring a tender heart as God made changes in my life that tore into my soul. God had given me back my heart, opened my eyes to my life, and wrestled me into his arms. I am changed and changing. I am reminded that the journey to peace and wholeness begins with a connection to one's own heart.

And the peace of God, which transcends all understanding, will guard your hearts and your minds in Christ Jesus.

PHILIPPIANS 4:7

LMP

Messy Situation

As late afternoon melts into early evening, the house seems to settle into a rich peace that calms a mother's heart. For just a few moments, motherhood feels like I always thought it should. My little ones are in the nest, home from school and extracurricular activities. The aroma of dinner cooking is wafting through the house as I turn on lights, bringing a glow to our dusky rooms. I feel the day's tension dissolve as I absorb the soft music playing in the family room. Upstairs the kids are tackling homework and making phone calls, with their own choice of background music. I revel in the "homeyness" of the moment. My children are safe in my castle. Peace.

Then we hear the undertones of a subtle rumble. The garage door. He's home. While no one mentions it, tension is instantly felt, and the peaceful moment is over. The dad is home. He's not a mean man. He doesn't abuse us. He just has expectations we can't seem to fulfill.

As he walks through the door, even before he puts down his briefcase, the litany begins. "Whose shoes did I trip over in the hall?" "Is there a reason every light in the house is on?" He sets down his briefcase and heads upstairs. I overhear him greeting his children. "Pick up those clothes! You're not going anywhere until this room is clean!" Mr. Neatnik, the perfectionist husband-father, has arrived, and it's time to shape up!

After observing this nightly scene and its effect on our family, I gently told my husband how I feared for his relationship with our children. The only common ground shared between him and his kids was tension about messy rooms. If something didn't change, he would end up with no relationship with his children. Saddened by that thought, he asked for a solution. I suggested he consider the kids' rooms as falling under my jurisdiction; if agreeable, he was simply never to mention their rooms again. Bedrooms might not be as neat as he liked (and he might have to look the other way when he walked by their doorways), but he might be able to save the relationship. It worked. Now, years later, he enjoys a warm, mutually respectful relationship with his adult children. He's convinced we salvaged their relationship from its path to destruction—just over their messy rooms.

Over the years a myriad of issues may sidetrack us from the real issue of relationship with our children. But before we let an issue rob us of relationship, let's remember the importance of a lifetime of relationship with our children.

[Parents], do not embitter your children, or they will become discouraged.

COLOSSIANS 3:21

RGM

Eternity in Our Hearts

Several years ago my parents bought an old house that had been the estate of an elderly couple who had lived there for over fifty years. They bought the place "lock, stock, and barrel"—everything from furniture to teaspoons. We gave away, threw away, sold, and kept a lifetime of possessions. We never met the couple whose lives we were invading; but by the time the house was cleaned up, fixed up, and placed back on the market, we felt we knew them well.

I often wondered what they would have said if they could have returned from the other side of eternity to find us up to our elbows in the relics of their lives. Would they mind that their hand-carved, walnut end table now sits at the end of the couch in my living room? Would they be bothered by the fact that my mother sets their dining-room table for our family dinners? I don't think so. I think they would have far more important things to say to us. A perspective looking earthward from heaven would be hard to contain, and yet, from the other direction, an earth-to-heaven perspective somehow eludes us.

It has been said that we no longer live under heaven. Perhaps we live only under sky. We have forgotten this world is not our home. We live as though this is all there is. We subtly or not-so-subtly teach our children to achieve, acquire, and accumulate all they can in life. We invest in IRAs, mutual funds, and penny stocks as though they can somehow change this world into heaven itself during our golden years.

I tremble when I think of what we may be teaching our children about heaven, even if by default. I see cartoons with elderly people in bathrobes and halos sitting on clouds watching the events of earth. One television commercial shows a celestial switchboard operator screening God's calls. And frankly, if heaven is anything like the sets of some of the Christian television programs I've seen, I'm going to pray that God will find a new interior decorator before I get there.

A friend of mine once said that when she thinks of heaven, she thinks of the warmest, most intimate conversations she's ever shared with friends over a cup of tea at the kitchen table. Deep sharing, tender words, honesty. Heaven will take that kind of intimacy and multiply it beyond our wildest imagination. In heaven we will know and be known. No hurts, no shame, no limits.

Ecclesiastes 3:11 tells us God has set eternity in our hearts. He's placed a hope deep within the center of our being for connection to something larger than us, something eternal. I want that eternal connection. I want to teach my children about it. I want to live in a world under heaven.

He has made everything beautiful in its time. He has also set eternity in the hearts of men; yet they cannot fathom what God has done from beginning to end.

ECCLESIASTES 3:11

LMP

Quality of Life

It was an ordinary September morning in our town. Moms were shuffling their kids off to school. Workers were sipping steamy coffee in the traffic, which inched them closer to the next paycheck. Amy was enjoying her morning run before her college biology class, stowing her notes for the quiz in the palm of her hand. Drivers who passed by admired her youthful fluidity, her strength and vitality, her confident stride. Everything changed as a passing vehicle veered out of control and collided with Amy's present, as well as her future.

An ambulance rushed her wrecked body to immediate medical attention, saving her life, but a coma held her in its paralyzing grip. Amy's parents arrived from South Carolina by the time I visited the ICU waiting room. I'd never met Amy or her family, but I found myself drawn into their story. I, too, had a vivacious college-age daughter who jogged before morning classes. Different campus, different state, same mother-love. I had little to offer—just my mother-heart. The more I learned about Amy, the more she sounded like my daughter: a pianist, an athlete and hiker, a youth camp counselor, a beautiful and independent lover of life.

When Amy emerged from the coma, she couldn't hear, speak, or move. In the months and years since, Amy's mother and sister have devoted themselves full-time to her care and recovery. Instead of questioning God with "why this?" Amy and her family have used this experience to share their faith in God's goodness.

Every time I look at Amy's picture on my refrigerator door, I think of my daughter, full of life, personality, energy, and athleticism. I wonder how I would handle seeing so much stolen from her. How could they be thankful?

On the first anniversary of the accident, Amy's family returned to our town to celebrate God's goodness to them and thank the hospital staff and local churches who had supported them through the trauma, and for Amy to attend school (in her wheelchair) with the boy who ran over her. Amy's wobbly attempts at walking with a walker were meant to be cause for celebration. She held a chalkboard so I could write brief messages to her, forming words as best she could with a mouth that had been paralyzed and a mind that had lived in a soundless world for over a year.

It isn't fair! I screamed inwardly. Tears were in my eyes, and yet a smile was on her face. What's wrong with this picture? How could she let go of the grief and resentment over loss and injustice—when I couldn't? She had lost her quality of life! Or had she? I was the one who had mixed up the idea of quality with ability to move and accomplish. Amy had a quality of life I couldn't touch. I sensed she'd discovered a contentment and intimacy with God I've only glimpsed.

You will show me the path of life; in your presence is fullness of joy;
at your right hand are pleasures forevermore.

PSALM 16:11, NKJV

RGM

Happiness Is ...

My fifteen-year-old and I were on the way to the mall when one of those glorious, unexpected sacramental moments seemed to fall from nowhere.

"You know, Mom," Michael said in an unusually pensive fashion, "if someone were to tell me I could either stay a teenager or go back to being a kid, do you know what I would do?"

I thought for a moment. Here was a kid whose teen years were going pretty well for him. He was second-string quarterback on the football team. He had made the varsity baseball team as an eighth-grader. He had friends in every high school in town and never lacked for companionship, male or female. But I decided to go with the flow of the conversation. "No, Michael, what would you do?"

"I would go back to being a kid."

I was more than a little shocked, but before I could say anything, he went on.

"I loved my childhood. I loved being a kid."

In a world where repressed memories and tell-all exposés abound, such words are music to a mother's ears. And they were coming from my second child, the one whose baby book contains his name, birth date, and the hospital-issued Polaroid. The one who wore hand-me-downs for the first five years of his life. The one whose care was entrusted to a nanny at the age of six months so I could go back to work.

My personal stats on this one were way below the mark of perfection. I was a working mom. I didn't take off the whole first year of his life as I did with his brother. I let him go to sleep with the television on. I let him eat sweets, and I didn't punish him when he drew a mural on his closet wall. He had more stitches than Frankenstein and fewer hours of my time than he deserved. But in spite of my slipups and misdirection, he remembers a happy childhood.

Michael remembers dressing in camouflage and playing war with his neighborhood buddies. He remembers home-run derby in the backyard and football in the front. He remembers sitting alone in his room playing with his "men" for hours. He remembers turning off all the lights for our "dinner and a movie" family time.

He also remembers a few spankings but admits now to deserving them. He has a vivid memory of almost severing three fingers in a bicycle chain, among other accidents, but such events seem to be a normal course of life to him.

If I could write the definitive *How to Raise a Happy Child*, some of the chapters would have to be, "Accidents: Your Child's Other Teacher," "Mothering From the Workplace," "Kids Need Space Too." Go figure. Maybe the book should have only one chapter: "Do the Best You Can, Learn All You Can, and Love More Than You Ever Imagined." That just might do it.

> Above all, love each other deeply, because love covers over a multitude of sins.
>
> 1 PETER 4:8
>
> LMP

Little Idols

Rachel dreaded moving away from her family. Jacob, her husband of six years, was employed by her father, but after twenty long years of her father's cheating schemes and repeated salary cuts, it was time for a job change. When Jake told Rachel that God was directing him to return to his hometown, her counsel was that of any wise wife. "So do whatever God has told you."

Secretly they made their moving arrangements and packed their belongings. While her father was away on business, Rachel removed some of his tiny household gods from his home and hid them in her luggage. These most valued possessions provided the last remnant of predictability in her life. But she couldn't tell Jake, who listened only to Yahweh. The little idols would have to be her secret.

Even though this story is told in Genesis 31, the reality is that little idols are hidden in our lives too. We may be like Jacob, unaware of their presence, or we may be like Rachel—not willing to give up familiar habits, routines, and priorities.

Anything that demands a position of priority in our lives qualifies as a household god. Any activity that distracts us from a lifestyle of worshiping the living Lord has become a household altar. Any attitude enslaving us to things of this world has become a worthless "little" idol, easily concealed in the busyness of demanding lives.

As conscientious parents, we willingly serve our children's best interests—providing them with all the opportunities we can and supporting them in all they do. We give them lessons, coaching, and computer programs. We pay for equipment, registration fees, and special camps. We take them to practices, watch their performances, and wait for them backstage and outside locker rooms. We sacrifice family vacations, our own social lives, and Saturdays. We become quite accomplished at saying no to anything that might conflict with our children's activities. Yet, in our single-mindedness, have we become enslaved to a distorted sense of "good parenting"—a household god which distracts us from choosing God's best?

We humans are capable of building altars to all kinds of gods—our career, our materialism, our reputation, our house, or even church work. All these can become consuming distractions from living a life of worship to the living God who desires our undivided hearts. The trap that ensnares so many of us parents, however, is the subtle servitude to our children's activities. When this idol takes over our home, we fail to teach our children how to make responsible choices. In a home that's an altar to the living God, parents make intentional choices toward meaningful, God-honoring priorities. Each child is a gift, each activity is a choice, and each home is an altar. Whom do you worship with your choices—little idols or a great big God?

"All right then," Joshua said, "destroy the idols among you, and turn your hearts to the Lord, the God of Israel."

JOSHUA 24:23, NLT

RGM

Road Trip

Bekah and I love traveling together. Whenever we can find an excuse, we jump in the car for a road trip. We have been known to stretch a three-hour drive into a seven-hour, antique-shopping adventure. We've even managed to make air travel something we look forward to. Give us an exit row, a diet soda, and a transcontinental flight, and we're good to go. At journey's end we always relive, replay, and enjoy.

About twenty-five years ago, my college roommates set out on a journey across the country in a little Triumph TR7 whose muffler was wired on with a coat hanger. Their eventual destination was California, but they had no idea when they would get there and didn't really care. They put their wheels on I-40 and headed west. Where they would go tomorrow depended only upon where they landed today. They had a wonderful, carefree time—no responsibilities, no schedule, no pressure, just the journey. And they *did* reach their destination—eventually.

Some of us cannot imagine enjoying the journey. As we feel tossed about by life, just as my roommates were on their cross-country adventure, we don't know where we'll be tomorrow until we land somewhere today. Admittedly, crisis does that to us. An unexpected illness, a loss of employment, a job transfer—life has lots of ways of slamming us around. But what if life feels like a crisis every morning? What if every morning brings with it that "Where-am-I-and-what-day-is-it?" kind of panic? Or what if it's just the opposite and you wake up knowing that today you're in the exact same place as yesterday, the exact same place you'll be tomorrow, and nothing in either direction seems worthwhile? Life doesn't seem to be a journey. It's a force to be reckoned with.

In the Old Testament book of Haggai, God sends a message to the Hebrew people who were living their lives without purpose, without direction. "Give careful thought to your ways," he says. The Hebrew word for "ways" in that verse means "journey" or "path." Give careful thought to your journey. Examine your life. Take a look at where you are, where you've been, and where you're headed. Hundreds of years ago Socrates said, "The unexamined life is not worth living." I believe he was right. The unexamined life is not much of a journey. Take some time to "give careful thought to your ways" today. With a good sense of direction, a desired destination, and unlimited flexibility, you might just find you can really enjoy the ride.

Give careful thought to your ways.

HAGGAI 1:5

LMP

Life Made Easy

Mornings! I just don't do them well. Droopy-eyed and noncommunicative, I enter the world in slow motion, not ready to relate to anybody or anything for a couple of hours. My husband, on the other hand, is ready to discuss his morning jog, the weather forecast, and the day's business. Our two children are also divided on the issue. One complains about the choice of cereals, while the other can hardly find the refrigerator. Somehow we manage to survive mornings in the kitchen without strangling each other.

One morning, however, I was startled from my grog as I went through the robotlike motions of fixing a peanut-butter-and-jelly sandwich for Ben's sack lunch. I stood barefooted in my white terrycloth bathrobe at the counter, and that's when I saw it—with my own two half-open eyes. It was right there on the lid of the grape jelly jar—the answer to every mother's question. A folded pamphlet, hardly bigger than a quarter, read: "Make your life a little easier!"

I wanted to shout for the world to hear, "I found the answer!" Wide awake now, I peeled the little folded paper off the lid—ready to receive the revelation that would revolutionize my life. Inside I found the answer: "Quenchade Ready-to-Pour Juice."

So the next time I'm supposed to be in three places at one time—Quenchade! Next time I'm neck-deep in fund-raiser details for the kids' school, wanting to be at my child's track meet, needing to prepare for a Bible study I'm going to lead, and needing to pack for a weekend trip, I'll just pull out the Quenchade.

Oh, that we could simplify life that easily. But life isn't easy. Nor can it be made easy with the flick of a magic wand. Let's face it: Life is hard for everyone.

When Susan wakes up every morning to face another day with her son, Gordon, who needs a respirator, feeding tubes, and a wheelchair to survive, do you think Quenchade helps? When Celeste puts her teenage daughter on a plane to attend a boarding school for the deaf, can I comfort her with a little grape juice? Anne's husband left her for another woman. Deena's son was picked up on drug charges and is in jail. Maggie is addicted to her depression meds. Cyndi doesn't know how she'll pay this month's bills, much less the medical bills that have accumulated. Looks like I need to buy Quenchade in bulk form!

We all know there's no magic potion. But as we struggle with life's complexity, we often complicate it with guilt. We're disappointed in ourselves, and we think God must expect more of us too. But here's the good news. If in your messy, complicated life all you can do is hold on, God is pleased with you that you're not giving up!

Let us run with perseverance the race marked out before us.... Consider him who endured such opposition from sinful men, so that you will not grow weary and lose heart.

HEBREWS 12:1c, 3

RGM

Children of God

My friend Lisa, like so many of us, lives in a home with a revolving back door. Lisa is the mother of two teenagers, Susan and Will—both gifted athletes. Lisa's family life is ruled by the iron hand of her children's schedules. Games, meets, two-a-day practices, traveling. Lisa and her husband deal with overlap by the divide-and-conquer approach. But Lisa is the one who often feels divided and conquered.

Lisa always dreamed of long heart-to-heart talks with her daughter and of possessing the trusted confidence of her son. Her life, however, leaves little room for talking and trusting. But Lisa's greatest concern goes even deeper. Her bruised heart has watched as both Susan and Will have developed a sense of self that is totally dependent upon their most recent athletic performance.

Susan is a competitive diver. Little golden divers sit perched atop hundreds of trophies lining every wall of her room. Will's six-foot-seven-inch frame leaves little doubt about his sport. He's been the tallest and the best on every basketball team since pee-wee league. If all goes well his senior year, he'll have his pick of scholarships. Susan and Will's dad is every coach's dream and every coach's nightmare. He never misses a game or a meet, and he often shows up for practice. He knows every twist and spring in Susan's performance and every squeak of Will's shoes on the court. His expectations are high, and he's rarely disappointed.

Conversations between Lisa's kids and their dad consist of stats, scores, and game analysis. When it serves his purpose, he'll flavor their discussions with such phrases as "God-given talent" and "being a Christian example out there on the court." But for the most part, Lisa's children have a relationship with their dad based upon their athletic performance. For Susan, her dad should be her protector, her champion. For Will—his role-model, his hero. Instead their dad is their biggest fan, their greatest critic, and the definer of their sense of self.

Late one night as Lisa walked past Susan's door, she heard pillow-muffled sobs. Practice that day had been particularly grueling. Susan was exhausted, overwhelmed, and terrified. Her team was counting on her to master a particular dive that would be their ace-in-the-hole for that year's competition. But it wasn't happening. She just couldn't get it.

"What will I do, Mom? What happens to *me* if I can't nail that dive?" In that moment everything Susan believed in, trusted, and had confidence in was falling apart. No dive, no Susan.

Lisa wrapped her arms around her daughter's weary heart. With tears she whispered, "Susan, don't you know that God doesn't read the Sunday sports section? Your heavenly Father desires a relationship with you based upon who he is and not on what you do. He has given you an incredible gift, but more important he gives you his love. His love, not your gift, makes you who you are—his beautiful child."

How great is the love that the Father has lavished on us, that we should be called the children of God.

1 JOHN 3:1

LMP

Simple Details

The phone rang on a Saturday morning just as my arms were loaded beyond capacity with dirty laundry. Everyone but me was either not home or asleep so I had to answer. I shuffled across the room doing a Hansel and Gretel routine with dirty socks. Leaning into a face full of dirty boxer shorts, I caught the receiver just before the answering machine clicked in.

"Hello."

"Hello. May I speak to Mrs. Linda Page, please?"

"This is Linda Page." This had better be good. Spit—spit—boxers again.

"Good morning, Mrs. Page. How are you this morning?"

I thought, *Do you really want to know?* But I said, "Fine."

"Mrs. Page, my name is JoAnn and—"

"How are *you*, JoAnn?"

"Excuse me?"

"I said, 'How are you, JoAnn?'"

"I'm fine. As I said, my name is JoAnn, and I'm with your cellular phone service, and I'm calling this morning to offer you detailed billing for an additional $1.97 per month."

"Detailed billing?"

"Yes, for only $1.97 a month, you'll receive a bill detailing each number you called, the time of day and the exact duration of the call. It will really simplify your life!"

I began laughing hysterically.

"Excuse me, Mrs. Page?"

"I'm sorry, but you *did* say this would simplify my life, didn't you?"

"Yes, ma'am."

"You're going to send me far more information than I want

or need, and it's going to simplify my life?"

"Well—"

"Do you know that last night during the Braves' game I learned the name of the player who is ranked seventh this year for hitting a single in the bottom of the ninth with runners on second and third?"

"Huh?"

"Would you like to know who that is?"

"Well, no, but—"

"Do you know it cost five thousand dollars per square foot to build Trump Towers?"

"I don't even know where Trump Towers is."

"Neither do I. JoAnn, my brain is filled with entirely too much useless information."

"I have a headache."

"Thirty-one. That's how many name-brand pain relievers are on the market for your headache."

"You're kidding."

"Yes, I am. But you didn't know it."

"Mrs. Page, may I assume you're not interested in the detailed billing our service is offering you today?"

"JoAnn, you may assume I need to know what day it is and who needs to go where when. I need to know how much milk we have, where the only pair of scissors we own is located, and approximately what time the air conditioner serviceman might come today. I don't need to know who I called on my cell phone last month. What was last month anyway?"

Just then a voice from the other room called, "Mom, the dog is chewing on the coffee table again!" Now that's a detail I can use!

Take my yoke upon you and learn from me, for I am gentle and humble in heart, and you will find rest for your souls.

MATTHEW 11:29

LMP

128

Significant Endeavors

Up-town girl. You been living in an Up-town world."

Mary and I bellowed out our respective harmonies to the Billy Joel song on the radio. I swayed and leaned on her kitchen counter while she stirred a jar of spaghetti sauce into her browning hamburger. (I don't remember where the kids and husbands were, but we were cutting loose since nobody was around to tell us to act like grown-ups.)

Mary was the coordinator of the gifted program at my kids' school. She was upbeat, enthusiastic, energetic, and stimulating—in a word, fun. She was the kind of person who made you feel gifted and creative whenever you were with her. She introduced me to George Winston's piano music, as well as the freedom to think in a smothering small town. (We nicknamed it "Stepford," and we were the "Stepford Wives," because the pressure to conform became comical at times.) I haven't heard from Mary in fifteen years, but I will never forget her or one concept in particular that came from all our hours of chatter.

It evolved from a conversation about how much we both detested the game of Trivial Pursuit. We invented a replacement game that would be worthy of people who truly valued their time. We called it "Significant Endeavors." This creation of our imagination would probe meaningful questions about life, rather than asking for irrelevant facts about unimportant places, events, and things. We never took our idea to market, but the idea continues to challenge me as I make my day-to-day choices. Is my life one of significant endeavors? Is *anything* I'm doing really significant?

As a follower of Christ, the only measure of significance is his.

The only unit of measure is eternity. The question ever before me is this: What is the eternal significance of this use of my time? Of this decision? Of this investment of my emotion and energy?

Giving timeless worth to each day I live is really not so impossible. It means devotion to the only everlasting things I know: God and the souls of human beings. Sometimes "eternal significance" is difficult to discern, but often I can envision how someone's eternity might be affected by the way I live my day. I can anticipate how God could use me to esteem my child with some focused time, share a truth with a confused friend, or support a person in need.

Life isn't a game. But there certainly are many questions, and the question of each moment is this: Am I choosing to invest myself in the eternally significant? The answer could mean the difference between a life of trivial pursuits and a life of significant endeavors.

Set your mind on things above, not on earthly things.

COLOSSIANS 3:2

RGM

Faith Floats

I often wonder what Noah would think if he could see himself in today's world. He has become a fashion icon, a decoration, a cute little fuzzy-faced, Santa Claus-type image. Wallpaper borders and baby blankets show his smiling face surrounded by cute little animals standing on the deck of a tiny boat. Children sing songs about "Father Noah" and wear him on T-shirts. He's a popular old fella, and I wouldn't have us do away with any reminder of his value to the world. But I fear we have diminished a spiritual giant to a smiling, happy, floating zookeeper.

Genesis 6:9 describes Noah as a "righteous man, blameless among the people of his time, and he walked with God." He was a righteous man living among the unrighteous, a man of peace in the midst of violence, a man who walked alone with God. Noah was the only man of his time whose heart wasn't constantly thinking of evil. He was a square peg, a misfit, an object of ridicule, and a giant of faith.

Noah was a "preacher of righteousness." I think of Noah sometimes when I see "Crazy Joe," a local character who walks around downtown preaching his heart out to no one. I wonder if Noah's neighbors called him "Crazy Noah" as he spoke the word of truth. I wonder if they elbowed each other as they walked by and did "Noah imitations" at the local gathering places.

Of course when we think of Noah, we think of the flood, animals, and the world's longest boat ride. When we see his happy little face painted on a lampshade in someone's nursery, we don't think of the man who walked with God for six hundred years before the flood began. We don't consider how he obeyed God in "holy fear" of things not seen. He built a boat on dry land, he preached without a conversion, and he walked into the ark and closed the door on the world as he'd known it. He must have heard the violence of God's judgment being carried out. Surely he was haunted by visions of his neighbors being swept away by rushing waters. Somehow the happy zookeeper image ignores many sobering aspects of what Noah was called to do.

It seems that the world in which we're raising our children is not so different from the one Noah knew. Violence and murder splatter the front pages of our newspapers. Christians are portrayed in the media as buffoons. Young people of faith are ridiculed and even killed for their beliefs. Christians are square pegs, misfits, nonconformists. Yet we desire for our children to take on this identity, knowing full well that as surely as Noah was called upon to live for his faith, our children might be forced to die for theirs. In living and dying, it's Noah-like faith that keeps us afloat.

> By faith Noah, when warned about things not yet seen, in holy fear built an ark to save his family. By his faith he condemned the world and became heir of the righteousness that comes by faith.
>
> HEBREWS 11:7

LMP

Turbulent Waters

Amidst the happy chatter at the dinner celebrating my parents' anniversary, I couldn't resist asking my parents a big-picture question. My motive was one of genuine curiosity and a desire for a perspective from almost fifty years of marriage.

"What were the most difficult years?"

I expected tales of financial struggle or havoc wreaked by jealousy, employment frustrations, or even long-hushed marital stresses. I was surprised at my mother's reply.

"It was when each of you kids went through junior high school."

Puberty is hard on everyone in the family. I remember my own children's passage from prepubescent confusion into early adolescent turmoil. Complicating the process at my house was the chaos created because the genders didn't experience it simultaneously. The sixteen months separating my daughter and my son suddenly seemed more like four years. My eleven-year-old daughter was thinking about dating, while my ten-year-old son was still playing with toy cars. Then there was the insecurity of changing classes at school, teachers who demanded more and coddled less, and that terrifying peer pressure. Hallway conversations at school carried a fascination with sex, drugs, tobacco, and shocking language. Are we surprised it is a difficult age?

Things at home began to change too. Loud music. Alien designer clothes and hairstyles. Bedrooms that looked like tornado-struck rummage sales. Endless phone calls. A new vocabulary. Had we unknowingly been "beamed" to another planet and been given alien children as an experiment?

How did we survive those turbulent times? We did it *together*. Like white-water rafting on Tennessee's churning Ocoee River, we knew we couldn't let them jump ship, hoping we'd reconnect with them at the end of the rapids. Upholding the relationship was vital. Communication was critical. Listening was as important as talking. And some of our best conversations took place in the car and in the bedroom after lights-out. (I seemed to listen better when I was driving or lying beside my teen in the dark, where I wouldn't get distracted by his or her personal expressions of hairstyle, makeup, and clothing.)

More important than establishing rules, we chose to teach principles. We set limits, relentlessly talking about *why*. We listened to their music and watched their movies, constantly discussing values and truth. We set values-based boundaries on clothing, continually discussing how our appearance affects others. We subscribed to call-waiting and gave our kids plenty of phone time because it was safer than letting them out of the house! Privileges were granted or withdrawn, based on the respect shown and how deep the well of wisdom within each child.

We were involved in their choices, their friendships, their dreams. We invested our time, energy, emotion. And should our family face more white-water rapids in the journey ahead, we will not be intimidated. We'll know how to ride it together.

If one part suffers, every part suffers with it; if one part is honored, every part rejoices with it.

1 CORINTHIANS 12:26

RGM

Make Us Truly Grateful

A nd, Lord, make us truly grateful. Amen."

So ended the prayer of the chaplain at a banquet I was attending. Before me was a meal of more roast beef than I could imagine consuming, green beans with red peppers and almonds, a twice-baked potato with all the trimmings, fresh tossed salad, a gigantic roll, and cheesecake with strawberry topping. I remember wondering if he really knew what he was asking. I remember wondering how many of us in that huge banquet hall were indeed grateful for the feast set before us. I remember wondering if I was prepared to handle it if his prayer was answered. What would it take to make me "truly grateful"?

In a world where self-sufficiency reigns, gratitude can be a rare visitor to our hearts. Gratitude is a matter of perspective. On my desk at home I keep a picture from the newspaper of a starving, crying, Sudanese child. His head seems out of proportion to his tiny, frail body. He is little more than skin stretched over skull, ribs, and limbs. His mouth is open in a cry, but there are no tears. A body must have sufficient water to produce tears. Beneath the picture I've taped the word "Perspective." I can only imagine the things for which his mother would be "truly grateful."

We who have so much, spend so little time in gratitude, but I believe we're making progress. Lots of women these days are keeping a gratitude journal, a simple daily list of things for which they're thankful. In mine I like to record my gratitude for one thing, one relationship, one act of kindness, one attribute of God, and one experience of beauty. A recent entry reads like this:

"I am grateful this morning for my waterbed, for its warmth, its coziness. I am grateful for my student Josh, whose deep needs make me a more compassionate teacher. I am grateful for the cyber-card of encouragement Carol sent me yesterday. I am grateful that God's love is unfailing even when I fail so often to see it. I am grateful for the aroma of some undefined spring flower that captured my senses as Bekah and I jogged up Bascom Road yesterday."

One thing, one relationship, one act of kindness, one attribute of God, one experience of beauty. Gratitude seems to open my senses to the multitude of gifts in the world around me. My perspective is changed, founded in truth, and I am on the path toward becoming truly grateful.

Give thanks in all circumstances, for this is God's will for you in Christ Jesus.

1 THESSALONIANS 5:18

LMP

When in Drought

Tennessee is having the biggest drought in decades. At summer's end the landscape looks more like October than August. Thirsty trees are dropping their leaves, crops are withered, and the dehydrated soil is crusty and cracked. Weather reporters count the days, while town folk join the farmers in praying for rain.

My life has had periods of drought too. There were some long dry spells of missing my family, when job relocations took us so far away that family gatherings were impossible. Gratefully, my thirst for family was watered by caring church families in those faraway places.

In a couple of towns, however, I suffered a "community" drought. I thirsted for a community of individuals who loved and cared about each other. Only by my own persistence in reaching out to others did I find refreshment.

Then there were "teaching" droughts—those seasons without sound biblical teaching. At first I didn't even know I was wilting. I would sit in a church, week after week, month after month, unchallenged to apply God's Word. I would attend gatherings of Christians where, instead of edification, I received friendly conversation, gossip, or invitations to go on guilt trips. I've come to realize there's really no reason for a Christian in America to live in such a desert. Scriptural teaching and encouragement are readily available to those who thirst for truth—through local churches, Christian broadcasting, or local Bible studies.

While no drought is enjoyable, the thirstiest I've ever been was in a "friend drought." Those times when there seems to be no one to share life with. In one such drought I cried and hollered at God for three years, pleading with him to provide me with just one trustworthy companion. Self-doubt found its way into the cracks of my parched being, as I wondered what was wrong with me. Finally I became convinced of the quenching truth that if Jesus was my only friend in this life he would be enough. Grace rained down from heaven and filled me with a new enthusiasm for living. And soon God even filled the seat beside me with a friend.

No doubt, the most terrifying drought is feeling estranged from God. You can't seem to pray. You can't feel his presence. You can't seem to make yourself read the Bible. You wonder if he's really there. You wonder if you're really a Christian. Our Father promises to make himself known to those who truly seek him, so, when in drought, keep seeking. The journey through the desert will take you deeper into your soul than grazing contentedly on lush green hillsides.

In contrast to the withering foliage in my yard, I've found droughts to be unlikely seasons of growth. My wellspring of hope and trust in the Lord has sustained me. And at the end of the struggle, the shower of grace has never tasted so sweet.

[She] will be like a tree planted by the water that sends out its roots by the stream. It does not fear when heat comes; its leaves are always green. It has no worries in a year of drought and never fails to bear fruit.

JEREMIAH 17:8

RGM

Family Soul

❀

It happened every time. They came in pairs. They came one by one. They came in groups. Families with barefoot children. Women in housedresses. Old men speaking in hissing tones around teeth-clinched cigarettes. They all came to sit on my grandparents' porch and listen. They came because the music drew them.

The people of the tiny community of Luray, Tennessee, would know that the McNatts were having a family gathering when my grandparents' yard began to fill with cars. Tables and chairs were set beneath the trees, tablecloths fluttering in the breeze. Giant tubs filled with ice and bottled drinks tempted thirsty little mouths. The women scurried in and out of the house bringing food by the plateful, bowlful, and basketful. Slamming car doors would bring my cousins and me running around from the backyard to see who was arriving. A grand day was in the making.

Through all the scurrying, fly swatting, feasting, and reuniting, the townspeople waited in their homes. They knew the morning's madness would settle into the afternoon's calm. And the music would begin.

No one would announce it. My uncle Melton would sit down at the upright Steinway in the living room and plunk out a few notes as though checking to make sure the piano still worked. In the back of the house, instruments were being uncased. One by one, uncles and cousins would walk into the room, instrument of choice in hand. Seemingly from nowhere someone would play a few introductory notes, and music would happen. After each song, both the players and their audience expressed satisfaction in quiet murmurs of approval. Center stage would shift from one player to another. My grandfather's fingers would fly up and down the strings of his banjo. One cousin would rattle the walls with a concerto, while another soothed our souls with jazz. The living room became a concert hall, the front porch a mezzanine.

The strains wafting from the windows and doors of the tiny frame house were such as could only be heard in music halls and nightclubs in cities far away. The townspeople came because the music drew them. But far more than melodies poured from my grandparents' house. Spilling from every opening was the soul of a family. Our knowing and being known was enveloped within the music. From fingertips and lips came the expression of the deepest part of us.

The soul of a family will find a way to make itself known. It wafts from the kitchen in the aroma of apple pie. It dances on the laughter of children, in the storytelling of old men. It settles softly into shared tenderness. The soul of our family sang its anthem for all who wanted to hear.

The people came to sit on my grandparents' porch and listen. They came because the music drew them, but what they heard was our family's soul.

I will sing and make music with all my soul.

PSALM 108:1

LMP

Wait Training

Spiritual peer pressure. That's what I was feeling as I sat in the circle of women who met weekly for Bible study and prayer. Kathy was directing children's ministries at her church. Mitzie was meeting weekly with teen girls for a breakfast Bible study. Barbara was speaking at women's retreats around the state. I felt like a spiritual nobody. With the aroma of baby wipes still on my hands, I sat among these ministering women—clueless.

Here I sat—willing, able, and available. *Here I am, God; send me. I want to be used to accomplish something significant.* I listened for his instructions. Nothing.

I couldn't believe he would pass up this opportunity—an eager servant, a willing heart. Didn't he hear my offer? *Lord, just say when, where, and what you want me to do.* Nothing.

Could he want me to wait? Was there a purpose for this time of inactive service?

Wait, Lord? Perhaps I should have told you I'm not good at waiting. It's not one of my gifts!

We've all been through various levels of "wait training." Wait until your father comes home. Wait until you're older. Wait until you're out on your own. Just wait until you're paying the bills yourself. Then there was waiting for the cute guy to ask you out. Waiting for him to pop the question. Waiting until we get married. Waiting for a promotion. Waiting for a baby. Waiting for the baby's father to get home. Waiting for the baby to get over something. Then some smarty-pants would add, "Just wait until she's a teenager!"

Now it seemed I was being told to wait again—this time by the very One who called me to surrender every aspect of my life to him. I felt like a favored doll placed back on the shelf. I guess that's why I've come to call these times of waiting "shelf time."

Over the years my life with Christ has been flavored by times of salty ministry, yet peppered with shelf times. Nevertheless I've come to realize that shelf time is not wasted time. It's often a time of learning and preparation, nurturing, and spiritual refreshment and replenishment.

As we yearn to use our gifts to achieve the spiritually significant, God may ordain shelf times in our lives, but motherhood is hardly one of them. With motherhood there is no shelf time, no interruption in ministry. The ministry demands are ongoing—with noses to wipe, wounds to tend, wisdom to be communicated. Even while we wait for God to use our unique giftedness in spiritual service, I'm convinced there is no higher calling, no ministry more spiritual than the one he has given us with our children. The wait training may only be a gentle command to wait until another time because, for now, your motherhood *is* your ministry.

> Yet the Lord longs to be gracious to you; he rises to show you compassion. For the Lord is a God of justice. Blessed are all who wait for him!
>
> ISAIAH 30:18
>
> RGM

What Would Jesus Do?

Everywhere I turn these days people are supposedly asking the question, "What would Jesus do?" The popular phrase is engraved, silk-screened, and printed on wearables, hangables, and stickables. As a teacher I must admit I find it more than a little troubling when a youngster, wearing multiple declarations of the pivotal question, talks back or deliberately disobeys me. I could become pretty arrogant about the whole thing, proclaiming, "If you're going to wear the name of Jesus on your arm—blah, blah, blah." But then don't I claim to have the name of Christ engraved on my heart? What's the difference?

The question is penetrating: What would Jesus do? What would happen if Jesus wrapped my life around his heart and lived my day? My life, his heart. How would my day be different? The deviations would begin as the alarm penetrates my brain. Jesus never hit the snooze button. He didn't bargain for a few more minutes of rest before going to be alone with our Father. If Jesus were wearing my life, I believe he would let me sip my hot cup of coffee as I curl the covers around me, enjoying my Father's morning embrace. His heart would rest there, delighting in what God teaches me before my day begins.

The heart of Jesus would greet my family with a holy kiss. I would send everyone out into the day with assurance that, no matter what the day contained, they would be loved and welcomed back home at its end. My workday lived by Jesus' heart would be a faultless balance of doing my job well and loving others. No procrastination, no complaining about someone else having it easier than I do, no milking an extra minute out of my lunch break, no hurtful sarcasm, no scratch-your-back techniques. My relationships with my coworkers would be satisfying, honest, and loving. Jesus' heart was never known to be wishy-washy either. Conflict resolution would be swift and sure.

If my life were wrapped around Jesus' heart, I would not be afraid. I wouldn't try to impress, to look good, to feel good. I would continuously forgive and constantly love. No grudges, no bitterness, no demanding of rights, no blame game. I would accept every soul as wounded and in need of the very heart that beats within me, even the souls of those who wound me. I would see before each and every person in my day a basin of water draped with a clean towel. He would bend my knees, and with my life I would do the business of his heart. My life—his heart.

He anointed us, set his seal of ownership on us, and put his Spirit in our hearts as a deposit, guaranteeing what is to come.

2 CORINTHIANS 1:22

LMP

A Little at a Time

How in the world did I get here? I was sitting behind the wheel of a jam-packed twenty-four-foot Ryder truck, with my daughter's Jeep in tow. Through the windshield I viewed a panorama of desert and mountains, a backdrop for the Welcome-to-California sign. It seemed like only yesterday she was riding her Big Wheel to the corner.

Mothering a child is like flying a kite. Letting go too fast or too slow means it won't fly. Too fast—it will take a destructive plunge. Too slow—it will never reach the heights. As any kite-flyer knows, the key is knowing your kite, understanding the wind conditions, and timing, always timing.

I remember the transition from crayons to magic markers, from cutting to gluing, from "Mommy, read this to me!" to "I can read it myself!" I remember the graduation from training wheels to two-wheeling. Bicycling to skateboarding. Slumber parties to proms. Giggles over the phone to dinner and a movie.

It's difficult for a mother to let the string out. What if my daughter gets hurt? What if my son can't handle the freedom? We fear the move to the next step because we love them so much. With every breath we breathe, we are instinctively concerned for their well-being. But if we hold them back, they'll never fly. Let it out a little at a time, Mom.

On the other hand, it's difficult to hold them back these days. They want to be older than they are. They want more freedom. They want more independence. It's easier to give in, pretend you don't care. It's their life anyway. Let them make their own mistakes. But if they crash at an early age, they may never fly. Let it out a little at a time, Mom.

I remember the weeks Bethany spent at Kamp Kanakomo; tears filled my eyes as I drove away. I'll never forget hugging her good-bye in her freshman dorm room; I didn't let her see my tears that time. Her life has been filled with new schools, new friends, new adventures. A little at a time, Mom. Now she's decided to move across the country to try her wings in a new career. The old kite string is stretched about as tight as it can go. My little-at-a-time kite-string philosophy prepared us both for her to fly. What joy in seeing her soar!

There is a time for everything, and a season for every activity under heaven: ... a time to scatter stones and a time to gather them, a time to embrace and a time to refrain.

ECCLESIASTES 3:1, 5

RGM

The Paralytic

Julie is a paralytic. She's the mother of three and the wife of a loving, kind man. On the surface their family seems as normal and all-American as apple pie, but Julie is a paralytic. Oh, she walks just fine. Her arms and legs work just as well as anyone's; nevertheless, Julie is a paralytic. She isn't paralyzed in her limbs. Julie is paralyzed in her soul.

Every morning Julie barely manages to roll out of bed and shuffle her children off to school. Most of their questions go unanswered. "Mom, where are my basketball shoes?" "Are you coming to my class party?" "Mom, are you OK?" Most people don't know that as soon as the children are safely on the school bus, Julie will pad back to her bedroom and make herself a cocoon of pillows and comforter. There she will read the morning paper while game shows mumble background noise on the television. Breakfast dishes piled high in the sink, Julie administers the anesthetic of distraction to her soul. Julie is a paralytic.

Jesus met a paralytic or two during his time on earth. Probably the most memorable was one that floated down in front of him as he was teaching in a home in Capernaum.* Four very determined and faithful friends lowered the man, helpless in his body and hopeless in his heart, down through a hole in the roof. Jesus, as always, saw the heart of the matter. He saw not just the crippled body, but the invalid heart of the man before him. Surely the man must have determined he deserved his body's condition. He must have spent his bedridden days repenting and regretting some sin in his life. Jesus was moved by the faith of the friends who brought him there. They knew

Jesus was the only rescuer for the body and soul of their friend.

Jesus spoke first to the gnarled and knotted heart of the still and twisted man before him. "Take heart, son—your sins are forgiven." What joyous words! What release! This man's soul must have gone leaping around the room! But Jesus wasn't finished. "Arise. Take up your bed. Go home." His words to the man revitalized the body wrapped around this soul set free. The man was made completely whole.

Julie's friends remember how she used to be—alive, energetic, loving, and gentle. They don't know it was her daughter's fourth birthday that injected the paralyzing venom into Julie's soul. They don't know that age four was when Julie's dad began to molest and abuse her. Julie's friends are simply determined to take up her bed and take her to Jesus. She doesn't always want to go with them. She would rather stay home than go for a walk, out to lunch, or shopping. But they keep calling, and she goes sometimes. Tile by tile they remove the roof and take their friend to Jesus.

Praise the Lord, O my soul, and forget not all his benefits—who forgives all your sins and heals all your diseases.

PSALM 103:2-3

LMP

*Mark 2:1-12

Patchwork

An enormous quilt hangs above my fireplace, warming the two-story room with its hues of rust and blue. Years ago, my friend Mary coached me through the careful selection of fabrics and the hundreds of hours of stitching that eventually produced this—my first quilt. The technique I used to piece together the quilt top required sewing long strips together, cutting, positioning, meticulously matching seams, and then more sewing to create the desired pattern. Only an experienced quilter could have foreseen how these linear strips of cloth would be transformed into a vibrant star made up of hundreds of diamonds.

How our lives and our children's are like my Lone Star quilt. Our lives are a carefully planned patchwork of multifaceted and colorful experiences. Convinced the Master Patchworker has a beautiful and unique plan for each of our lives, I still wonder about some pieces that don't seem to fit in my life. Then I remember that some of the most not-so-pleasing-to-the-eye fabrics can be crucial in creating a most pleasing effect in a finished quilt. Similarly, the ugly experiences of life are used by the Creator and Weaver of beauty to produce Christ's likeness in us.

The pieced design, like the patchwork of life experiences, provides the focal point. But the more crucial and time-consuming process often goes unnoticed and unappreciated—the process of hand-quilting the pieced quilt top to the other layers. Crucial because the underlayers give the quilt substance and purpose. Folks don't cuddle up under a flimsy single layer of pieced-together fabric scraps. That's because a quilt top alone lacks warmth.

In life, the experiences, rich with color and detail, come together to form who we are, but we need more. We need God to be our substance and give us purpose. Without him the experiences of our lives do not produce beauty, but a cold and messy reality. His presence provides the warmth, the weight, the depth.

As mothers we watch the weaving together of experiences in our children's lives, wanting them to encounter the depth and rich warmth available only through knowing God. He brings substance to their lives and gives purpose to their experiences—joyous or sad. I believe God designed motherhood to be the thread, woven through their experiences, constantly anchoring them, stitch by stitch, to the only One who can bring substance and purpose to their lives.

This is the painstaking part of quilting—and of motherhood, because it takes so much time and effort. Day by day we see very little progress. But with every encouragement, hug, reminder of truth, nod of approval, and tearful prayer, we can stitch another stitch closer to the beauty and purpose God designed for their lives. Let us never forget how critical we are in the creation of an extraordinary patchwork.

> "For I know the plans I have for you," declares the Lord, "plans to prosper you and not to harm you, plans to give you hope and a future."
>
> JEREMIAH 29:11

RGM

The Good Life

To say that my relationship with Bekah has stretched me would be an understatement. She has stretched my horizons, my creativity, and my legs. But the most unexpected stretch came on her final Friday as a resident of my hometown. The women of our church had planned a "girls' night out," but Bekah had planned a "stretch"—a stretch limo, that is.

Unknown to our friends and me, Bekah secured the services of the longest, whitest, flashiest stretch limousine around. She wanted us always to remember her last weekend in town. She wanted us to have the ride of our lives. She wanted us to have a taste of the "good life."

With limo plans made, Bekah began calling some of the women who would be going to our little party and offering them a ride. She didn't tell anyone they would be riding in luxury. I, along with three others, accepted her offer.

Several women turned down Bekah's offer to take them to the party. One of them thanked Bekah for the offer but said she wanted to drive independently so she could leave the party whenever she wanted. Another said she had dinner plans before the party and would probably be late as it was. One declined Bekah's offer, saying she might have to leave if her husband called for reinforcements with the kids at home. One refused because it was too far out of Bekah's way to pick her up. She just couldn't be that much trouble especially when Bekah had so much to do and so much on her mind and blah, blah, blah....

Their reasons were valid, perhaps, but interesting in light of their responses once they saw our arrival.

"If I'd only known!"

"Why didn't you tell me?"

Such were the reactions of those who had rejected Bekah's offer. Bekah offered them a taste of the good life. They settled for ordinary, for convenience, for autonomy. I wonder how many times I've been offered the good life but have chosen to live in habit or expedience. How many times has God said to me, "Linda, may I offer you a ride?" How often have I said no because I wanted to take my own car—be in control. Because my plans were made and couldn't be changed. Because I'm limited by others' expectations. Because I can't possibly matter that much to God.

God doesn't always offer convenience, comfort, or expedience. He simply calls and offers me a ride. He calls and offers me the good life. I wonder how often I've passed it up.

I came that they might have life, and have it abundantly.

JOHN 10:10, NAS

LMP

Vain Babblings

He's so vain!" The big-man-on-campus seemed to be the topic of my daughter's animated phone conversation with a girlfriend. Ah, yes, the word *vain*. A word we use for *other* people—those who are obnoxiously self-centered. Conceited movie stars. Muscle-builders who walk with a strut. Chicks whose body language demands the attention of all eyes. Rarely do we see ourselves as vain.

But when Jesus taught about praying, he told us not to use "vain" repetitions. Me—self-centered? My prayers—self-absorbed?

Vain also means empty and useless, fruitless and futile, devoid of value and worthless. Vain describes my attempts to turn cartwheels or make cream puffs. Vain appropriately describes my efforts to break lifelong habits or keep New Year's resolutions. Surely it doesn't describe my conversations with God—or does it?

Jesus' list of "top ten prayer no-nos" includes "babbling on" like those who think they'll be heard if they use lots of words. I admit my husband has insinuated—once or twice—that I've been guilty of babbling. The implications are that my words are thoughtless and meaningless. Ouch! So why would Jesus suggest such a thing about my prayer life? My prayers—babbling? Hmm, perhaps I need to re-examine my prayer patterns.

Many of my prayer patterns were set when I was a child. *Dear God, please bless Granma and Granpa and all the children in the world.* What do you mean—meaningless? Even if I didn't know what I meant, I thought you did, Lord!

Other prayer patterns were modeled by those in leadership in the churches I attended. *Lord, be with us today, Lord, as we meet in your name, Lord; and, Lord, be with everyone, Lord, who isn't able to be with us today, Lord.* OK, I guess I notice a *few* unnecessary words, wrapped around a concept of asking for something we already have.

Please give us nice weather for the picnic, God. Does that sound self-absorbed? Well, I don't pray that one very often.

Lord, heal Mary Jen and help her have a successful surgery and help the tumors go away. Now what's wrong with that? What do you mean you might want to use the tumors to grow her spiritually and draw her closer to you? I didn't think about what *your* will might be.

Lord, help me pass the exam. Help my child win the competition. Help us not have car trouble. Please transfer my boss. Move my neighbor. Change my husband. My prayers are often vain, self-centered, and empty because I haven't even considered what the Sovereign Answerer of prayer might have in mind in all these situations.

How's this then? *Lord, help me see my world as you see it. Help my heart beat with yours. Help me want what you want—hearts yielded to your will, lives submitted to your lordship. And, by the way, I'm ready for you to begin with mine.*

And when you pray, do not keep on babbling like pagans, for they think they will be heard because of their many words.

MATTHEW 6:7

RGM

Gotta Have It

About thirty years ago, the highway department of our state was in the mountain-moving business. Interstate 40 was under construction, chomping its way through the Appalachian Mountains of East Tennessee. Traveling the old, winding, soon-to-be-obsolete highway in those days, you could hear the dynamite blasts as massive chunks of stone and earth were relocated from their natural, earthly habitat. Gigantic machines gnawed and chewed and carried away any mountain that stood in the way of transportation progress.

History tells us that during Jesus' ministry, Herod was also in the process of moving mountains. He was constructing for himself a city which would testify to his greatness. His workmen moved dirt one shovelful at a time. Such was the setting when Jesus said to his followers, "If you have faith as small as a mustard seed, you can say to this mountain, 'Move from here to there,' and it will move."

Sometimes now, as we wind our way toward our favorite vacation spot in the mountains, I find myself with a smile on my face. I try to imagine a construction worker, wearing hard hat and boots, hurling a mustard seed at the granite mountainside and running for cover. But Jesus meant what he said about mustard seeds and mountains. Scripture tells us of some powerful mountain-movers.

Faith is a supernatural confidence that God's promises are true. It is founded upon what God has done and moves us toward what he is about to do. People of Scripture used those promises to move some massive mountains. "By faith," says Hebrews 11, the people of the "Hall of Faith" brought down summits.

Noah hammered, sawed, and swiped on tar, by faith and faith alone. No clouds threatened his world; no thunder rumbled of approaching doom. Only God's promise and instruction moved his hands to work. He moved a mountain of lumber, a mountain of hay, and a boatload of animals. And, even more, he stood immovable himself in a deluge of persecution. As the fountains of the earth swept away the evils of man, the voices of hate were silenced. Noah floated safely in his ark built by faith.

Abraham moved mountain after mountain in his lifetime. He is probably most famous for climbing a mountain carrying with him the knife that would sacrifice his son. He believed the promises of the God who had given him his son. "We'll be back for you," he told his servants as he and Isaac climbed the hill of sacrifice. Abraham moved a mountain of fear and doubt.

In the New Testament, Peter was given a vision that shattered his personal worldview. His faith sent him into a world he would have otherwise considered unclean, the world of the Gentiles. Peter moved a mountain of prejudice.

Are our mountains so different? Hatred, prejudice, persecution, violence, fear, doubt. The mountains of Scripture are the mountains of the millennium. May God bless us with mustard seeds to move them.

> I tell you the truth, if you have faith as small as a mustard seed, you can say to this mountain, 'Move from here to there,' and it will move. Nothing will be impossible for you.
>
> MATTHEW 17:20

LMP

The One to Whom I Answer

❀

"I can't believe you're not letting me go to the most important event in my life!" my dramatic teenager shouted loud enough for the neighbors to hear. She stomped up the stairs and slammed her bedroom door. I had lost the mother-of-the-year contest again.

First, let me clarify: Bethany was not a spoiled-rotten, disrespectful child. She was no stranger to the word *no*, but obviously she had never learned to like it.

My mind flashed back to her toddling years, when she probably thought "No" was her first name. "No, Bethany, don't touch the outlet." "No, Bethany, don't climb on the chair." "No, Bethany, don't take Benji's truck."

As she grew, so did the complexity of guiding her. "No, Jennie may not spend the night." "No, you may not ride your bike to school alone." "No, you may not watch that movie."

By the time she was a teen, mothering her was getting pretty complicated. Bethany's strong will was exhausting me. Her protests could almost convince me *I* was the one being unreasonable. "Why *can't* I subscribe to that magazine?" "ALL the other parents are letting their kids go!" "You just don't want me to have any friends!"

Didn't she realize it would be easier for me to say yes? If I could just let her do what she wanted, I wouldn't have to ponder and pray over how best to guide her. I wouldn't have to face her verbal opposition. Our home would be quieter. I could save my energy, and it might even be fun to be a mother who is popular with her kids. But I just couldn't take the easy way out. I was accountable for more than simply making her happy. So I explained it ... again.

"God is holding me responsible for loving, protecting, and guiding you. You may not like how I do it. I may not do it perfectly. In fact, I'm sure I'll make some mistakes. But I have to answer to God, so what *you* think of my parenting is not what really matters."

I'm not sure Bethany was always in a frame of mind to understand what I was saying to her, but it was the truth. When I was worn down by her protests and tempted to give in, I reminded myself that her acceptance and approval were not my objective. In my desire to have a great relationship with my children, facing their displeasure with me remains difficult—even as they grow into young adults. This is especially intimidating for moms whose only fulfilling relationships are with their children.

As a parent I must remember to whom I answer. Though we parents are motivated by a desire for our child's highest good, there is an even higher accountability. This challenging standard we must remember: God has entrusted this child to my care, and my responsibility is to Him.

> But remember that you must give an account to God for everything you do.
>
> ECCLESIASTES 11:9d, NLT

RGM

Hat-in-Hands Humility

I was twenty-something when my husband and I joined the ranks of DINKs. That's socio-economic talk for Double-Income-No-Kids; new house, two cars, and a country club membership. I tried to fit the mold, but my heart kept breaking it.

I remember standing by the putting green with my friend, Becky, at a country club in a nearby town. Our husbands were playing in the club's summer golf tournament, and we had joined them for the Saturday night barbecue. Becky and I didn't know anyone, so we were standing alone talking, trying to be inconspicuous in this southern country club scene. Tan men in brightly colored shirts intermingled with squeally women in coveys of pastel sundresses. I just wanted to eat my share of pig meat and go home.

Suddenly someone shouted to one of the "men in brights" who was being especially loud and obnoxious. "Hey, Bob, you've got company."

Walking across the fairway of the eighteenth hole was an elderly black man. He was dressed in a pair of unfaded overalls and a clean white shirt. Probably the best he had. He walked slowly, watching every blade of grass under his feet, only looking up often enough to be sure he was headed in the right direction. He held his straw hat in both hands in front of him.

The man named Bob let go a string of expletives and walked out to meet the old man before he came too close to the crowd. Their conversation was brief. The old man never looked up. He stepped back, nodded in gratitude and walked away just as he'd come. The story was that the old man's wife needed to go to the hospital. He came to ask Bob, his employer, if he would loan him enough money to ensure she got the care she needed. Bob may well have been kind in his exchange with the old man, but when he returned to his crowd he was anything but. Of course he'd take care of the old woman. "Don't I always take care of my n——s?"

My jaw dropped to the floor, and my twenty-something-year-old heart ran after the old guy. I looked into the crowd, searching for another pair of sympathetic eyes. I wanted to walk up to Bob and use a few of his own expletives on him. I wanted to shout to everyone there that I wasn't like them. I felt more like the old man than part of Bob's moneyed crowd.

I've thought about that old man a hundred times since. I remember Jesus' words about poverty and poverty of spirit. That old man showed me both. Poverty of spirit means that before God I have no resources of my own. I, too, must go to the only One who can take care of me and ask humbly for help. May I constantly live in poverty of spirit and the power of hat-in-your-hands humility.

Do nothing out of selfish ambition or vain conceit, but in humility consider others better than yourselves.

PHILIPPIANS 2:3

LMP

Close Encounters

I couldn't wait to share my good news with Linda. I dialed her number, and my heart sank a little as the dreaded electronic voice of her answering machine kicked into its monotone greeting: "Please-leave-message-after-beep."

I'd have to settle for talking to a machine. "Linda, it's me. Have I got something to share with you! Call me when you get home."

It's truly a gift from God to have a friend with whom to share life's joys and sorrows. How much more reassuring that the Creator of friendship is *totally* accessible! No waiting room, no answering machine, no appointment necessary!

Sure there's the scheduled weekly rendezvous, when hopefully corporate worship brings me to a close encounter with God. But I'm thankful I don't have to depend on my pastor or worship team to orchestrate my meetings with God.

In solitude and quiet I can meet him in Scripture, study, or meditation. He can be my constant companion in an ongoing conversation throughout the day. And my soul is refreshed by inspirational teaching, a weekend retreat, or music—ah, music—with or without words.

Yesterday he met me in my garden, my hands caked with dirt. And today he was there for me at Wal-Mart when I needed self-control. We often bump into one another in the midst of affirming or encouraging words. And I ran into him the other day just as I was pounding nails into a Habitat for Humanity house.

I feel his hugeness as I gaze upon the ocean or over a snow-capped mountain range. I recognize his command over the universe as I witness a sunrise, a sunset, or a star-studded night sky.

I enjoy his company on walks in the woods and bike rides in the country.

I've seen him in the tears of a grieving friend. In the truth-telling of my repentant child. In the laughter following a shared story on a porch swing. I've touched him in the clutch of a crying child and in the tender hug from a friend. I've celebrated him at births and new beginnings. I've known the comfort of his embrace in times of grief and loss.

He's with me as I exercise, as I work, and as I relax. He's in my tears over Hallmark commercials. In my awareness of how rich my life is. In my surrender of pride. He helps me let go of my fears, my anxiety, my injured memories, my need to control. He helps me let go of my children—releasing them to him.

The Bible says he inhabits our praise, so I frequently visit him there. I feel his presence when a friend trusts me with her heart. And I know he lives in the love I have for those I cherish. He and I agree, as I pray for their highest good.

Close encounters of the divine kind are daily opportunities. We don't have to wait for Sunday morning!

> Yet a time is coming and has now come when the true worshipers will worship the Father in spirit and truth, for they are the kind of worshipers the Father seeks.
>
> JOHN 4:23

RGM

Out of Control

"W hy are so many people eating out tonight?" I wondered as we circled the parking lot for the third time. "It's Thursday. We're supposed to be avoiding the weekend madness." The fourth time around revealed an opening between two minivans in the next row, but when we turned down the aisle we could see a woman standing cross-armed in the parking place. She had staked her claim and was defiantly shaking her head no to me or anyone else who thought they might park there. I was so appalled I drove on and found a vacant spot on my fifth time around. A gentleman in a big blue luxury car wasn't so easily deterred.

We were walking toward the restaurant when we heard the commotion. Mr. Big Blue Luxury Car and Mrs. Defiant were screaming at the top of their lungs. He threatened her, and she dared him. Pretty soon her husband arrived to capture the parking spot, but Big Blue was in his way. He used his horn as an offensive weapon, bringing out both the restaurant manager and the police. I don't really know what happened after that, but none of the parking lot screamers came inside to eat. They probably had all lost their appetites. They probably had ulcers. They probably didn't sleep well that night. All in the name of a parking place. All because of passion gone out of control.

I believe we should live lives of passion. I believe we are called to pursue our passions. Passionate living is a vital response to the tenderness of God's heart. But passion out-of-control springs from the flesh, not the heart. Larry Crabb has said, "To the degree that you haven't found God, your passions are out of control."

Our misplaced, carried-to-extreme, out-of-control passions point us toward the places in God's heart we haven't visited. If my passion is anger, I haven't found God's peace. If my passion is unforgiveness, I haven't found God's forgiveness. If my passion is bitterness, I haven't found God's goodness. If my passion is physical relationships, I haven't found God's soul. If my passion is material things, I haven't found God's treasure. If my passion is success, I haven't found God's plan for me. If my passion is relationships, I haven't found God's presence. If my passion is myself, I haven't found God.

I don't know the underlying passion of the woman in the parking lot. Anger, maybe; bitterness, perhaps; or maybe her husband was in poor health and needed to be close to the restaurant door. Whatever it was, her passion, expressed in her venomous words, was misplaced at worst, extreme at best, but clearly out of control. "To the degree that we haven't found God, our passions are out of control."

> You will seek me and find me when you seek me with all your heart.
>
> JEREMIAH 29:13

LMP

Heart Gifts

Breathless in nervous excitement, I watched my friend open the gift representing weeks of thought and selection. Would she be as pleased and surprised at my creativity as I anticipated? It seemed unlikely my gift would offend or insult her, but it had happened before.

Gift giving is sticky, complicated business. Most of us have our own unspoken, even unconscious set of gift-giving rules. Price limits. Appropriate occasions. Reciprocal obligations. Gift-to-gift value comparisons. My plan to give a gift begins in my heart, but by the time I remember all the rules, I'm tired.

Whenever I allow myself to be enslaved to obligations and expectations, the bondage robs me of any joy in the giving. Often I become paralyzed by the fear that my gifts will be rejected or misunderstood or criticized or used as a reciprocal standard to be matched. Even playing it safe and submitting to another's rules, I enjoy no guarantee that my gift will bring delight.

Gift giving, at its best, is an art of the heart. A gift is intended to be an offering which lovingly communicates: "Thank-you." "I'm sorry." "I'm glad you were born!" "I was thinking about you while we were apart." In its purest form, gift giving is motivated not by rules, but by an overflowing heart.

Browsing in a flea market I think of my mom and dad; I purchase an unusual dish from yesteryear to add to their collection. Enjoying a beach vacation I collect shells to take to a friend who's in my thoughts. Leafing through a book in a bookstore I jot down a quote to share with my book-lover friend.

A gift is a medium to carry a message. Its substance is of

little importance. A purchased item or a personal creation—fresh-out-of-the-oven sweet rolls, a photograph, a quilt, a flower, a card, a phone call, a letter. A few words scribbled on scrap paper may be worth far more than an extravagant purchase because of the love it communicates.

Gift receiving, too, is an art, it seems. Great gift receivers don't measure the worth of the gift by the cost, but by the intended message of love. They don't compare their gifts to the ones others receive. They never imply the gift is untimely, impractical, or not useful. Such receivers elevate the joy of giving.

As I ponder my feelings of rejection and disappointment over a gift not joyfully received, I think of how God must feel when I don't receive his gifts well. So many times I've let him know I had something else in mind and expressed my disappointment in what he's given me. How I must have hurt him! For I know my gift Giver has lovingly chosen every gift for me. Oh, that we would learn to receive all his heart gifts well! And as we learn to receive, may we set others free to give from the heart.

Each [woman] should give what [she] has decided in [her] heart to give, not reluctantly or under compulsion, for God loves a cheerful giver.

2 CORINTHIANS 9:7

RGM

Peace on Earth

"I wonder what's going on?" I said to the boys as we waited to turn out of our neighborhood. Traffic was inching along at a snail's pace on a street where Nascar wanna-be's practice their racing skills. The snail's tail passed in front of me, and I took my place in line. I could then see what was holding everything up. Cars were backed up behind a truck pulling a Christmas parade float, no doubt on its way to a parade in a nearby town.

It was, after all, the first week of December, and it suddenly struck me that I hadn't been feeling very festive. I'd hosted the family Thanksgiving dinner and pushed pretty hard to get things ready. The Thanksgiving turkey was nothing more than a soup-bone now. The cranberry sauce was only a tablecloth stain. A new holiday was lurking out there, just waiting to be conquered. Now this bouncing little float with flashing foils was unexpectedly arousing the Christmas spirit in me.

I knew I was going to get the eye-rolling thing from my boys, but strains of carols ringing in my head were bursting to get out. I opted for "Joy to the World."

Unfortunately my solo rendition was interrupted when the little red sports car in front of me poked its nose out into the oncoming lane. Approaching traffic forced him to reconsider. The driver of the little red sports car retracted its nose and pounded his fist on the dash. A few seconds later he tried again. Same poke, same retraction, worse reaction. This time he began gesturing wildly. He looked like a fire-and-brimstone preacher driving home his climactic point, but somehow I don't think those were "preacher words" coming out of his mouth.

The boys had overcome their humiliation over being in the car with a caroler. They fixed their attention on our unhappy antecedent. We watched intently as he failed a third time to escape the traffic snarl. This time brought resolve. He slumped in his seat and stroked his bald head vigorously. He had accepted his fate. His pace was at the mercy of a Christmas float.

After about a mile of putting along, two lanes dispersed into four, and the little traffic knot untied. The boys and I just couldn't help but watch him as he burst into the passing lane. He must not have been in as big a hurry as we thought. As he passed the little float, he took the time to raise a chosen finger in vengeful salute. The little Christmas float responded in silent, glittering gold. "Peace on Earth, Good Will to Men."

Sometimes the distance between good and evil is no more than a traffic lane.

In your anger, do not sin.

EPHESIANS 4:26

LMP

Follow Me

"Follow me."

Compliance to these words has taken me to some places I wanted to go and to some that brought only regret. I've followed others down twisting, turning paths that spun my life out of control. I've found myself at a dead end, face-to-face with the one who led me there.

I remember following a playmate across a forbidden ditch, a boundary line of my childhood. The impending consequences did not deter my choice to follow. I remember playing "Follow the Leader" but finding it no fun unless I was in front. I will never forget following my classmates as we crossed a stage and graduated into life. Twice in my life I have followed a nurse down a sterile hallway to a labor room to bring into this world a little one who would follow me—at least for a while.

"Follow me" is a command not to be taken lightly. Jesus voiced it, and, for his disciples, obedience meant their lives would never be the same. Following him they would no longer seek fun, finances, or fish. They would seek the hearts of people. They did a lot of leaving behind in order to follow Jesus. They left their fishing and tax-collecting; their wives and their children; their homes and comfortable nights of sleep. Left behind were their security, their identity, their responsibilities, all familiarity, and life as they'd always known it. They followed Jesus from Jerusalem to Sidon, from plenty to poverty, from death to life, life to death, and back to life again.

As a believer, I am compelled to consider Jesus' words, "Follow me." What do they mean for me as a wife, a mother, a friend, a teacher? In so many of my life roles I am considered to be a leader. But in every role and position I hold, my primary concern is following. Following involves choice. To follow I must choose not to lead. I must choose to relinquish the head of the line. Unlike the disciples I haven't been required to leave my family, my job, my friends, my home, and my life. I am simply asked to follow as I lead.

"Come, follow me," Jesus said, "and I will make you fishers of men."
MATTHEW 4:19

LMP

At Home

My Missouri roots were calling me back—back to where my history began. My soul stirred with a mixture of anticipation and apprehension, the inevitable emotions prior to a class reunion. As the miles whizzed by, so did the Tennessee cotton fields in full bloom, the churning Mississippi River, and the rich delta farmland of the Missouri "boot heel." Tiny farm towns and melon-laden flatbeds slowed my pace, allowing for a neighborly wave here, a friendly nod there. Past the bottomlands of sorghum, soybeans, and corn, the landscape dramatically changed to dense forests, spring-fed rivers, and rugged hills. I trailed behind laboring logging trucks through the steep and unsympathetic terrain—a rocky topography where only trees could grow.

It felt good to be back in the arms of my Ozark hills once more. Here the clear-water streams meander through the wooded hills, engraving their signature on the land with caves and spectacular bluffs. Here the rural folk are friendly and unpretentious, decorating their yards with all the old cars they've ever owned. As I approach my hometown of Rolla, I feel comfortable—like a foot feels in a well-worn shoe.

My people are no longer here. My family and most of my friends are gone. Yet everywhere I look, I see myself. There I am in the little girl skipping out of the library, in the teenager giggling with friends outside the corner drugstore. This is "home" for me because this is where I started being me.

Home for me, however, has come to mean more than a place of origin. Home means acceptance and shelter, unconditional love and support. In Anna Quindlen's book *One True Thing,* the central character, Ellen, admits after her mother's death, "I was sick in my soul for that greater meaning of home that we understand most purely when we are children, when it is a metaphor for all possible feelings of security, of safety, of what is predictable, gentle, and good in life."*

As an adult I've discovered home, not in places, but in people. When I find someone who understands my heart and accepts me unconditionally, I know I'm safe. I am "at home." In a noisy, untrustworthy world this person offers a tender refuge—a place I can be myself. My soul feels comfortable, like a tired foot in a soft slipper.

The other day, as I sat in a café with a friend, it occurred to me I'm a home for others in my life. With teary eyes my friend told me how I'd become a safe place for her—a place where she could risk being herself. A place where she is unafraid, where she's assured my responses will spring only from love and acceptance.

We all need a place to call home in this world. What a privilege to know that I—as a friend, a mom, a wife—can be just such a place, where others can feel safe, secure, and free!

I would hurry to my place of shelter, far from the tempest and storm.

PSALM 55:8

RGM

*Anna Quindlen, *One True Thing* (New York: Dell Publishing, 1994), 284–85.

Hopeless Hearts

One Saturday morning, the aroma of fresh-baked bagels, mixed with that of rich, steaming coffee, lifted me out of my car and into the local bagel shop. In an olfactory stupor I almost missed seeing a couple of old friends of mine seated at a corner table. His face was buried in his newspaper and she blew ripples in her coffee, staring mindlessly out the window. Since I knew both of them were teachers, I granted them the right to be recovering from the same kind of week I had had.

"Everything going OK at school?" I asked them collectively.

"Same old, same old," he said, giving his paper a commanding shake.

"You wouldn't believe me if I told you," she said, turning her deadpan from the window to me. "Besides, what difference does it make?"

I began fishing around in my brain for something pleasant and clever to say, but she rescued the moment by asking how my year was going. I don't even know what I said, but I'm sure it wasn't clever. I couldn't concentrate on what I was saying for trying to find some sign of life in her eyes. They reflected no light, flashed no anger, offered no invitation.

I felt as though I had been released from a vise-grip as I ordered my coffee to go and made my escape. The expressionless eyes I had just encountered weren't always blank and emotionless. I knew this woman in college and graduate school. She was vital and energetic, someone I wanted for my partner on class projects. But now it seemed I had gazed into a soul without hope. Somewhere along the way, she had "grown weary and lost heart."

Most of us have said at one time or another, "My heart's just not in it anymore." The phrase brings about an acceptable exit from hobbies, volunteer work, even from a career. But my friend's heart seemed to have escaped her life. For her, tomorrow offered nothing but more of today's unpleasantness.

She wasn't angry. She was way past anger. Her soul was in a far more dangerous state—a state of indifference.

If our lives truly reflect what we believe about God, then my friend must have decided God is indifferent. She must have decided God doesn't care about the problems she encountered at school, the ones she was sure I wouldn't believe. She must have decided God isn't interested in her flat and passionless relationship with her newspaper-reading husband. She must have decided God's heart is like hers—detached, void of hope, and indifferent.

Little does she know that God's heart flutters with hope that she will return to him someday. Little does she know that he knows everything about her, from the ripples in her coffee to the ripping wounds in her heart. Little does she know that she is his passion, and he is her hope.

> May the God of hope fill you with all joy and peace as you trust in him, so that you may overflow with hope by the power of the Holy Spirit.
>
> ROMANS 15:13

LMP

Flying Solo

❈

"Squawk!" Pushed out of the nest again! A baby eaglet learns how to fly by being nudged out of the nest by the mother eagle. On the first flying lesson, poor little eaglet tumbles through the air—down, down, down. As he shrieks and squawks in panicked eaglet voice, the parent eagle flies along next to him, and just before the eaglet smacks into the ground the mother eagle swoops beneath him with giant wing and carries him back to the nest.

"Aaahhhh!" sighs little eaglet. "Safe again, back where I belong!" His panicked eaglet mind relaxes.

But then suddenly his world goes topsy-turvy again as Mama nudges him out of the nest with the tip of the wing that just rescued him. Over and over, the process is repeated until little eaglet finds wings of his own and learns to fly solo. For eighteen years this same process was going on at our house, and now our eaglet was ready to fly.

Our youngest was about to graduate, and everyone seemed excited—except me. Everybody wanted to talk about his future. What about mine? Wasn't it my world that was about to turn topsy-turvy now?

Years ago I'd gone through the normal stages of searching for significance as a "nonworking" mom. Let's face it—the full-time mother-thing leaves one yearning for affirmation, positive strokes, a sense of being appreciated, and any remote evidence of accomplishment. The rewards of motherhood are just so intangible, so long-term, so delayed.

Once I was convinced I had no more important job in the world than mothering these children God had given me, I could cope with the rest of it. The years without anyone saying, "You're doing a good job with your kids." The thankless meals cooked and carpools driven. No raises. No promotions. No vacations. Just knowing I was doing what God called me to do.

Now what? My nest would soon be empty. Where would I find anything half so significant in which to invest myself? I spent Ben's entire senior year asking God, begging God, to give me a new sense of direction. Should I start a new career? Should I go back for more schooling? Should I use my newly freed-up time to pour myself into volunteer work? I was restless and afraid—afraid of insignificance!

God's answer for me seemed to be, "Be still." He didn't give me a great passion to embark on any new and all-consuming endeavors. The only all-consuming endeavor he had in mind for me was to seek to live a life that glorifies and pleases him. Such is to be my passion, whether my eaglets are in my nest or flying over faraway cities.

Years later, my eaglets are flying high, my nest is empty, but my life is full. Full of people. Full of purpose and significance. But you know what? I still haven't found anything more fulfilling than teaching my children to fly.

Her children arise and call her blessed.

PROVERBS 31:28

RGM

Do-Overs

Things don't always go perfectly in a backyard baseball game. No umpires, no real pitcher's mound, no baselines. No coaches, no homerun fence, no dugouts.

One thing a backyard game does have is "do-overs." Do-overs come when something that simply cannot be reckoned with interferes with the course of the game. It might be a neighborhood dog, a three-year-old, or even somebody's dad deciding to get in the middle of things. "Do-over! That doesn't count! Do-over!" We can still hear our children's voices from the neighbors' backyard.

Sometimes in life you get a do-over. You get to glue it, erase it, transplant it, wallpaper over it, or serve it as a casserole. Most of the time, however, life stands firm as it is. Our words, our deeds, our choices scatter like feathers in the wind. No retrieving. No do-overs.

Erma Bombeck wrote a column not long before she died called, "If I Had My Life to Live Over Again." Many of the things she would do differently had to do with her children. Since both of us are on a fast train toward fifty years on this planet, we decided to visit Erma's idea.

Linda's Do-Overs: I would laugh more, play more, and sing more silly songs. My boys would remember more parks, playgrounds, poems, and picnics. I would teach them more about kindness than cleanliness. There would be more brushing and flushing than rushing. I would plant more whisker-brushed kisses on the cheeks of my teenage boys. I would close my book, my computer, and my thoughts of a deadline so I could listen to every detail of Michael's evening or Jeff's golf game. I would be less distracted and more present, less professional and more Mom.

Bekah's Do-Overs: I would laugh more and listen more, especially when they weren't talking. I'd step out from behind the kitchen counter or the ironing board to sit eye-to-eye at the kitchen table while they'd tell me about their day. I'd praise more and pick less. I'd take every opportunity to communicate my love and acceptance of them as persons, regardless of how I might disagree with what they do or wear or think. I'd have more one-on-one picnics with each of my kids. I'd go out on more dates with their father. I'd go on more family trips, even if it meant missing ball games and making the coach mad. I'd spend more time relaxing with my kids. Why were we always in such a hurry? I'd encourage them to be themselves, instead of trying to recreate them in my own image. I'd nurture an atmosphere where mistakes are the basis for learning, not judgment. I'd do fewer good things and more God-things. I'd pray more.

But life isn't a backyard baseball game. No matter what the interference, we really don't get do-overs.

The wise woman builds her house, but with her own hands the foolish one tears hers down.

PROVERBS 14:1

LMP/RGM

Reflective Parenting

"All right, young lady, you're grounded! And no telephone and no TV for a week!"

I cringed as my husband overreacted and pronounced the judgment. A week-long sentence—for me, as well as my daughter. The decree had been proclaimed; now the whole family would pay not only for my daughter's offense, but for a parenting error as well.

In a wave of emotion we parents have the potential to transform into tyrannical bullies. Conversely, in moments of weakness we may allow our children to do the unthinkable. Plagued by fatigue, we may give in to their demands or fail to discipline outright disobedience. Each of these scenarios is irresponsible parenting.

There are many reasons for the choices I make as a parent. Some are about getting my own needs met. "Go watch TV; Mommy's busy." Or "Go ahead and do what you want; I'm tired of reasoning with you!" Sometimes I just mimic the way my parents reacted to me. Sometimes I'm motivated by what other parents might think. Sometimes, just once in a while, I consider what is truly best for my child. It's called "reflective parenting."

I can easily miss the mark of reflective parenting. I could make rules for myself: "I'll never miss any of my kids' events." I could make my choices on auto-pilot, without thinking about the consequences: "It just seems like the thing to do." I could be driven by guilt or other pressures: "What will people think?" Or I could simply take the path of least resistance, choosing the easiest option—for the moment.

But reflective parenting cannot be regulated, dependent on innate responses, or yielded to external pressures. My most significant parenting will require making one wise choice at a time. On one day the highest good might be attained by sitting in the stands at the track meet or taking my daughter shopping or carpooling for the class field trip. But on another week or day the highest good may be attained by saying no to my child, to his teacher, or to her coach. Sometimes other things are more important. Many times my choice will not be understood.

But I have learned that, if I am to live with myself, with my God, and with the consequences, the best choices are well-considered choices. We spend more time cooking a well-grilled steak than we spend making a well-thought decision involving our child! The choices I make as a parent are worth the time, effort, and reflection it takes. Reflecting on God's will as revealed in Scripture. Reflecting on how the child will be impacted and influenced. Reflecting on my own motives.

Reflective parenting isn't easy or simple. It's good. It's good like God's Father-love for us. It's good like Christ's sacrificial love for us. It's good like the Holy Spirit's guidance that points us to rightness and always back to God. That's the kind of good parent I want to be.

The wisdom of the prudent is to give thought to their ways.

PROVERBS 14:8a

RGM

Moments

The loudspeaker interrupted my math class. "Mrs. Page, your son is on the phone." A tiny knot twisted in my stomach as I quickly arranged for my assistant to take over while I made my way to the office. I thought to myself how much simpler life was when my boys were both in elementary school and in the same building with me.

"Hello," I said, not certain yet which of my sons was on the other end.

"Mom, I need your permission to leave school and go home."

"For what?" I answered, wearing my relief like a downy comforter.

"Mr. Jones is sending me home to shave."

"You forgot to shave this morning?"

"Yes, ma'am."

"Yes, you have my permission, but tomorrow please look in the mirror before you go out the door." I hung up the phone and laughed quietly to myself.

It seemed an odd time for memory to overtake me. *Shave? Wasn't it just yesterday he was a soft-faced lap-crawler? Didn't I just recently hold him still and stroke his brave head as he took his eight-year-old booster shot? Couldn't we still fit in his bunk bed for one more reading of his favorite bedtime story?* No, my sleepyhead story audience now had a neglected five o'clock shadow. Those tender, nestled moments are gone, but how my memory retrieves their peace. I don't want to forget them. I pray that I didn't bypass them. May you capture your moments like fireflies in a jar. This little firefly was captured by my friend Jeanie Gushee on a rainy afternoon.

Rain Song

Raindrops make small white
Triangles of wet where they hit,
Bounce and dance on pavement
Beneath a matte, no-color all-day sky.
On a porch swing of a hundred-
Year-old house a mother sits
The central diamond in the
Diadem of family,
Surrounded by her jewels:
Little boy, and two young daughters,
And one daughter almost big as she.
They watch the rain and smell
The soaked-earth autumn scent, and swing,
And she sings rain songs to her people:
"Listen to the rhythm of the falling rain."
The swing creaks, and children chatter,
And probably jostle each other and tattle,
"Rain, rain, go away"—
And small hands pat her hair,
And she hopes memory never fades
Of how fond and daft and
Ravishing were these days.

Jeanie Gushee, 1999

But his mother treasured all these things in her heart.

LUKE 2:51b

LMP

The Unbowed Knee

She died satisfied. She had lived a long, full life. She grew up in a poor family, one of a dozen siblings raised to serve God and work hard. And work hard she did. As a child and young woman she worked side by side with her mother to care for the big family. She cooked, she sewed, and she cleaned.

Then she met her man. With an invincible love and deep-seated work ethic they began a life together. They took their children to church and Sunday school; they taught them Christian values through the week. Together they raised gentle and kind, responsible and caring children. Their daughters married gentle men. Their sons married kind women.

With the children grown, the larger part of life loomed before her. Family responsibilities, of course, were not over. There were grandchildren to cuddle and rock. There were aging parents to care for. Her many siblings had needs and expectations. She gardened and baked, sharing her goods with neighbors, church bazaars, and county fairs. She spent hours at the sewing machine, creating curtains and quilts and baby-doll clothes. Her husband loved her and encouraged her. Together they read the Bible every day and prayed for their family.

After nearly sixty years of marriage, her husband died, leaving her to face this world alone. In deepest sorrow she continued to read her Bible and pray daily for her children, grandchildren, and great-grandchildren. She read devotional books and listened to inspirational tapes. She went to church every Sunday.

Throughout her life she was known for her dedication to her husband and family. Neighbors appreciated her for all the kindnesses she'd extended over the years. Church members revered her for all the serving she had done. As an old woman she mentally patted herself on the back for living such a good life.

Certainly she had fulfilled every definition of the Christian woman. Or had she? She never prayed, "Lord, how do you want to change me?" She never pleaded with God, "Break my stubborn will, Lord. Make me the woman you want me to be." Change and brokenness were for those who sinned. And she was doing everything right.

She had always avoided small group Bible studies; those women got too personal! She never answered the application questions at the end of a Bible lesson or devotional; those must be for women who needed help. She never let anyone know she had any problems. And as for struggling with her attitudes or thoughts, well, she just didn't.

She had so much to be proud about that she found it hard to be humble. In fact, even though she used humble-sounding phrases, her underlying attitude was self-righteous and judgmental of others. She never saw her own sinful selfishness. She never bowed her knee.

That at the name of Jesus every knee should bow, in heaven and on earth and under the earth, and every tongue confess that Jesus Christ is Lord, to the glory of God the Father.

PHILIPPIANS 2:10-11

RGM

No Finish Line

On the wall in my laundry room hangs a poster—a surreal photograph of a lonely runner running down a desolate road with no end in sight. The words across the bottom read: "There is no finish line." The truth of these words has been etched deeper into my understanding with each year of my life.

Life *does* have its finish lines: sunsets, final exams, graduations. Project completions, retirements, book endings. But most of life is lived in the ongoing. Like the famous battery-driven bunny, we keep going ... and going ... and going.

Relationships (good or bad) go beyond the lines of disagreement, beyond miles and years of separation, even beyond divorce. Housework is never done! I can never say I'm finished reading the Bible and consider myself done once and for all with my spiritual growth. (Imagine hearing someone say, "Ah, it's so good to be finally done with all that growing and to be completely intimate with my heavenly Father!")

There is no bottom to my laundry basket, no final bill to pay, no ultimate letter to end all letter-writing. No end to my dental care, watching my diet, or attempting to stay fit. There are always more meals to fix, more floors to vacuum, more shirts to iron. More groceries to buy, more books to read, more gifts to give.

Serving others, loving others, serving and loving God. Rarely do any of these elements of living have pauses, much less endings. It should come as no surprise that motherhood is no mere eighteen-year contract. Once a mother, always a mother. Ask any mother who has grown children, any mother whose children have rejected her, or any mother who has suffered the loss of a child. There is no finish line to motherhood.

In the beginning we think we're signing up for a nurturing assignment that will be over in two decades. Little do we realize then how the mother-heart of love will be a primary part of our existence until we breathe our last breath.

Little ones grow up. They become independent. They leave us to live their own lives. But in our heart of hearts we love on.

We pray for them. We encourage them. We pray for ourselves as we continue to be a voice in their lives.

We learn well the unwritten, divine tenets of motherhood. Once you're a mother, your heart is never fully your own again. You're never able to think only of your own interests. You always know a strange incompleteness whenever your child is not with you, as if a part of you is missing. You forever recognize your own limitations and the necessity of trusting in God's faithfulness.

It's like breathing. Sometimes it's hard, but that doesn't make you want to stop. Riddled with heartbreak and joys, motherhood is a God-ordained merging of richness and responsibility that never ends. God designed the mother's heart to beat with an inextinguishable love like his. For there is no finish line.

Love never gives up, never loses faith, is always hopeful, and endures through every circumstance. Love will last forever.

1 CORINTHIANS 13:7, 8a, NLT

RGM

May the God of peace, who
through the blood of the eternal covenant
brought back from the dead our Lord Jesus,
that great Shepherd of the sheep,
equip you with everything good for doing his will,
and may he work in us what is pleasing to him,
through Jesus Christ,
to whom be glory for ever and ever.
Amen.

HEBREWS 13:20-21